NSTA Guide to
SCHOOL SCIENCE
FACILITIES

James T. Biehle
LaMoine L. Motz
Sandra S. West

NSTA Guide to
SCHOOL SCIENCE FACILITIES

Project Manager: M. Sheila Marshall

Editor: Suzanne Lieblich

Contributing Editors: Juliana Texley, M. Sheila Marshall

Contributors: Terry Kwan, Raymond E. Filipiak, Keith Verner

NSTA Associate Executive Director: Phyllis R. Marcuccio

Layout & Production: Catherine Lorrain-Hale
Book Design: Richard Curtis
Cover Illustration: Martha Peña Weiss
Stock Number: PB149X1
ISBN Number: 0-87355-174-5

Copyright © 1999 NSTA
National Science Teachers Association
1840 Wilson Boulevard
Arlington, VA 22201

Contents

Preface   **v**

Introduction   **1**

CHAPTER 1

Advocacy and the Planning Process   **3**
Empowering with Information 3
    Support for Good Facilities 4
    An Interpretation of the Standards 4
The Planning Phase 5
    Participants 5
    Planning Committee 6
      Curriculum Subcommittee 6
      Facilities Subcommittee 6
      Project Oversight 6
      The Planning Process 6
      Defining the Science Curriculum 7
      Evaluating Existing Facilities 7
      Determining the Nature of the Facilities 7
      Obtaining Approval and Financing 8
      Selecting the Architect 9
      The Design Phase 9
    The Role of the Science Education Leader 9
      Supervisory Roles 10
    Addressing the School Board 10
      Communicating with the Board 10
      The Presentation 10
Building the Science Facility 11

Charting the Path 11
    Time Line 11
    Construction 11
    Paying the Bill 14
      Developing a Project Budget 14
      Relocation 15
      Controlling Extra Costs 15

CHAPTER 2

Current Trends and Future
    Directions in Science Education   **17**
Standards-Based Programs 17
Integrated Curricula 17
Co-Teaching and Inclusion 18
Independent Projects 18
Secondary Courses 18
Instructional Methods 18
Technology and Tomorrow's Curriculum 19
Distance Learning 19

CHAPTER 3

Safety, Accessibility,
    and Legal Guidelines   **21**
Building for Safety 21
    Adequate Space 21
    Electricity 22
    Emergency Exits 22

    Gas 22
    Hot Water 23
    Eyewash and Safety Shower 23
    Storage Facilities for Students 23
    Storage of Hazardous Chemicals 23
    Ventilation 24
    Fume Hoods 25
    Fire Protection 25
    Other Factors 26
    Special Precautions for Seismic Areas 26
    Problems Specific to Renovations 26
ADA Guidelines 26
    Information Sources 28
Minimizing Litigation 29
    The Research Base 29
    Tort Law 29
    Best Practice 30

CHAPTER 4

Designing Facilities for the
    Elementary School (K–5)   **31**
Space Requirements, Room Design 31
The Multiple-Use Classroom 31
    Furnishings 32
The Specialized Science Classroom 32
    Furnishings (K–2) 32
      Sinks (K–2) 32
      Work Space (K–2) 33

Storage (K–2) 33
Display Space (K–2) 34
Utilities (K–2) 35
Lighting and Darkening Rooms (K–2) 35
Computers (K–2) 35
Furnishings (3–5) 36
Sinks (3–5) 36
Work Space (3–5) 37
Storage (3–5) 37
Display Space (3–5) 37
Utilities, Lighting and
    Darkening Rooms (3–5) 37
Computers (3–5) 37
Teacher's Space 37
Preparation and Storage Areas 38

CHAPTER 5

Designing Facilities for
the Middle School (6–8)   **39**
Grouping Facilities for Integration 39
Space Requirements 40
The Combination
    Laboratory/Classroom 41
A Flexible Room Arrangement 41
A Classroom Area and Fixed Workstations 42
    Furnishings 43
    Sinks 43
    Work Space 44
    Storage 44
    Display Space 45
    Utilities 45
    Lighting and Darkening Rooms 46

Computers 47
Workstations for Students
    with Disabilities 48
Teacher's Space 48
Preparation and Storage Rooms 49
Student Project Areas 51

CHAPTER 6

Designing Facilities for
the High School (9–12)   **53**
Grouping Facilities for Integration 53
Types of Science Rooms 54
Space Requirements 55
Separate Laboratories and Classrooms 56
The Combination
    Laboratory/Classroom 56
A Classroom Area and Fixed Workstations 57
A Flexible Room Arrangement 58
    Furnishings 58
    Sinks 58
    Work Space 60
    Storage 61
    Display Space 62
    Utilities 62
    Lighting and Darkening Rooms 63
    Computers 64
    Workstations for Students with
        Disabilities 65
Teacher's Space 65
Preparation and Storage Rooms 66
Student Project Areas 68

CHAPTER 7

Outdoor Facilities and Plant Windows **69**
Native Plantings 69
Models and Other Resources 69
Greenhouses 70

CHAPTER 8

Finishing Materials for Science Rooms **73**
Floors 73
Ceilings 74
Walls 74

APPENDIX   **75**

A: Solar Energy for School Facilities 75
B: Building for Safety in Secondary School
    Science Facilities: A Survey 77
C: Table of Critical Dimensions 84
D: Equipment 87
    Projectors and Screens 87
    Planning for Equipment Purchases 87
    List of Suppliers for Laboratory
        Furniture and Equipment 88
E: Sample Checklists 90
    Elementary Science 90
    Middle School Science 91
    High School Science 92
F: Photograph Credits 93
G: Glossary of Construction Terms 94
H: Bibliography 98

PREFACE

For almost 50 years, the National Science Teachers Association (NSTA) has been providing information to teachers and schools regarding science facilities and equipment. To provide assistance in the design of secondary school science facilities, the NSTA in 1954 published its first book on facilities, *School Facilities for Science Instruction*. This publication was revised and updated in 1961. Although the Association subsequently released several related pamphlets, it became evident by the end of that decade that an updated document was needed.

With new science curricula being published in the 1960s and early 1970s, supported by the National Science Foundation (NSF), a renewed interest and concern for updated and appropriate science facilities was created. In April 1970, NSF approved a grant to NSTA to study exemplary science facilities and identify emerging trends in facility design and use. The publication, released in 1972, *Facilities for Secondary School Science Teaching: Evolving Patterns in Facilities and Programs*, was a result of a project directed by Joseph Novak, of Cornell University.

In 1988, as NSTA president, I established the Task Force on Science Facilities and Equipment. The charge to this task force was to develop a publication or publications on instructional science facilities for elementary and secondary schools and to encourage and assist educational institutions in securing the best facilities possible for science instruction.

The task force was chaired by Ronald Converse, coordinator of K–12 science, Conroe Independent School District, Conroe, Texas. Other members were Dorothy Barton, curriculum coordinator, Beers Middle Elementary Science Program, District of Columbia Public Schools, Washington, D.C.; Tony Beasley, coordinator of K–12 science, Metro Nashville Schools, Nashville, Tennessee; Thomas Gadsden, director of science, K–12, Richardson Independent School District, Richardson, Texas; Ronald Maxwell, independent facilities consultant, Lake Leelanau, Michigan; Ronald Sass, professor of science education, Rice University, Houston, Texas; Victor Showalter, director, Center for Uni-

fied Science Education, Capital University, Columbus, Ohio; Jon Thompson, director, Kalamazoo Area Mathematics and Science Center, Kalamazoo, Michigan; Marlin Welsh, director of science, K–12, Shawnee Mission Unified School District, Shawnee Mission, Kansas; and Phyllis Marcuccio, director of publications, National Science Teachers Association.

This task force spent several years studying trends and directions in the design and implementation of elementary and secondary science teaching and learning facilities. They invited school districts to submit videotapes of their exemplary science facilities.

In 1992, a new NSTA Task Force on Science Facilities and Equipment was established, with myself as chair. This group met in Charlotte, North Carolina, and outlined a new beginning and direction for a publication on kindergarten through grade 12 science facilities. The members of this task force were Dorothy Barton, Tony Beasley, and Ray Filipiak, Sheldon Laboratory Systems; Jim Biehle, American Institute of Architects, Saint Louis, Missouri; Thomas Gadsden, Ronald Mazwell, Ronald Sass, Victor Showalter, Jon Thompson, Marlin Welsh, and Phyllis Marcuccio. This meeting produced a pamphlet, *Facilitating Science Facilities: A Priority*. This publication was a checklist for administrators and boards of education, and was disseminated via the NSTA journals and newsletters as well as through various elementary and secondary school journals and newsletters.

During an NSTA Convention in Phoenix, the task force met and established a working outline for the current publication, and several representatives from national science facilities manufacturers joined in the discussion of the outline.

Several task force members were then invited to write recommendations on science facilities for the National Science Education Standards (NSES). The result was the development of guidelines for elementary, middle, and high school science facilities based on NSES Program Standard D: Resources, and published in NSTA's three-volume publication *Pathways to the Science Standards*.

This *NSTA Guide to School Science Facilities* includes information about planning facilities design, budget priorities, space considerations, general room and laboratory design, furnishings for the laboratory/classroom, and much more. This publication represents the cooperative input of hundreds of hours and the effort of many individuals.

First acknowledgement and gratitude must go to the NSTA publications staff for all of their efforts and assistance in completing this guidebook. Special thanks go to Sheila Marshall, who guided us through this project, and to Suzanne Lieblich, whose expertise in editing assured us a fine product.

A large number of interested people submitted suggestions and references, and provided valuable reviews of the manuscript.

A deep sense of gratitude is extended to James T. Biehle, AIA, president, Inside/Out Architecture, Clayton, Missouri, for his untiring support, interest, and tremendous contribution to the writing of the publication. A special thank you is also extended to Sandra West, Juliana Texley, Terry Kwan, and Keith Verner for their outstanding contributions to the development of various parts of the manuscript.

This book could not have been complete without the support and assistance from several manufacturers of science facilities and equipment. Our special thanks to Victor Smith, Bubba Wood, and Raymond Filipiak, of Sheldon Laboratory Systems; Thomas Trapp and David Myers, of Sargent-Welch/VWR; and Rick Federico and Bruce Sanders, of Fischer Science Education. Additional thanks go to Martha Peña Weiss, of Pfluger Associates, Architects, Austin, Texas, for her contributions to the layout drawings.

The support and encouragement of many teachers, supervisors, curriculum directors, and other administrators of science education kept our task focused and moving towards completion of the project.

To Gerry Wheeler and Phyllis Marcuccio, thank you for the contributed counsel and ideas, as well as the administrative and editorial assistance.

To all of these and many others, the director and task force owe much for their valuable contributions.

LaMoine L. Motz
White Lake, Michigan
March 1999

NSTA Guide to
SCHOOL SCIENCE FACILITIES

INTRODUCTION

Through the National Science Education Standards, our profession has called for learning environments in which students explore, inquire, and construct their own knowledge about the physical world. Good science programs require the uniquely adaptable learning space we call a laboratory, as well as access to both indoor and outdoor space for research, nature studies, and reflection. Yet the vast majority of communities moving toward the Standards will find their progress limited by the facilities available in their schools.

Today, across the country, record numbers of school buildings are in disrepair. One third of our schools, which serve over 14 million students, need either extensive renovation or reconstruction, and another third have at least one major structural flaw, such as a leaky roof, outdated electrical systems, or dysfunctional plumbing (General Accounting Office, 1996, 3.1). Many of the remaining schools were planned without an understanding of what we now consider the requirements for a good science education. Between 1990 and 2004, the student population is expected to grow by 20 percent, and many communities will need additional or expanded facilities (U.S. Bureau of the Census, 1995, p. 151). The good news is that school construction is already on the rise in several states.

As we move toward the National Science Education Standards, we must accept the challenge of revitalizing both our science teaching and our facilities. The Telecommunications Act, which is helping to upgrade technology in schools, is one example of how federal legislation is assisting local communities and states in improving existing schools and building new ones.

NSTA believes that the science facilities in our nation's schools deserve a strong commitment and continuous attention. It is in science classrooms that students work, learn, and experience real science, using the tools and practicing the skills and habits of mind that encourage science learning. Students form their first and most lasting impres-

A high school science laboratory. (1)

sions of the importance of science there. The attention that our communities pay to good science classrooms is a measure of the level of our regard for science education.

The ideas and guidelines for remodeling and replacing facilities presented in these pages are compatible with the principles of the National Science Education Standards, which detail expectations for teaching and programming at all school levels.

Those who are planning facilities for science education will want to weigh their plans in relation to the requirements of the Standards and to trends in science teaching. The resulting facilities should serve both the present and the evolving science programs of the future.

The purpose of this book is to familiarize educators, administrators, and citizens with the stages of the process of planning for new and renovated science facilities and to provide specific, detailed information on many items and aspects of the planning and design phases. This information will also be useful to facilities planners and architects.

Regrettably, in some cases, teachers asked to join a planning committee serve only as token members. Yet, the active participation of science teachers and leaders is key to a successful project.

This book is designed to provide teachers, curriculum leaders, and administrators with a broad vision of the role of facilities in science teaching, as well as the background they will need to become valuable contributors to any facilities project team. It also reflects the most up-to-date research on best practice and environments for science learning. We hope that the book will help planning teams design effective spaces that meet their objectives for teaching and learning science.

LaMoine L. Motz

References

General Accounting Office. (1996, June 14). *School Facilities: America's Schools Report Differing Conditions* (GAO Report No. HEHS-96-103). Washington, DC: Author.

U.S. Bureau of the Census. (1995). *Statistical Abstract of the United States: 1995* (115th ed.). Washington, DC: U.S. Government Printing Office.

CHAPTER 1

Advocacy and the Planning Process

Empowering with Information

Science educators believe that students best construct their knowledge of the natural world in safe, secure, and stimulating learning environments. In order to achieve their goals, teachers, researchers, and planners must become advocates for the schools in which they work. The program standards of the National Science Education Standards (NSES) provide a strong foundation for advocating improvements in school science.

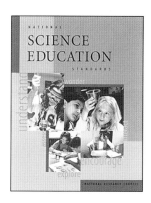

The National Science Education Standards. (2)

National Science Education Standards

National Research Council, National Academy of Sciences

Program Standards (Excerpts)

All elements of the K–12 science program must be consistent with the other National Science Education Standards *and with one another and developed within and across grade levels to meet a clearly stated set of goals.*

The program of study in science for all students should be developmentally appropriate, interesting, and relevant to students' lives; emphasize student understanding through inquiry; and be connected with other school subjects.

The science program should be coordinated with the mathematics program to enhance student use and understanding of mathematics in the study of science and to improve student understanding of mathematics.

The K–12 science program must give students access to appropriate and sufficient resources, including quality teachers, time, materials and equipment, adequate and safe space, and the community.

All students in the K–12 science program must have equitable access to opportunities to achieve the National Science Education Standards.

Schools must work as communities that encourage, support, and sustain teachers as they implement an effective science program.

SOURCE: National Research Council, *National Science Education Standards*, National Academy Press, Washington, DC, 1996.

A high school laboratory. (3)

This publication is a tool for teachers, science specialists, school teams, architects, and others concerned with planning, designing, and building exemplary science facilities for the youth of today and the future. The information in the chapters that follow is intended to empower teachers, schools, and communities to meet the challenge set by the National Science Education Standards.

Support for Good Facilities

One of the earliest, and often hardest, steps in the process of renovating or developing new science facilities is to convince the school community that change is needed. Given the tremendous pressure to expand and improve all kinds of educational facilities, it is up to science teaching professionals to become advocates for the resources and classroom environments they and their students require. And while administrators, school board members, and parents may initiate building programs based on their perceptions of space needs, it is important for educators to promote an understanding of the National Science Education Standards and their significance and to integrate these Standards into the decision-making process.

NSTA's Task Force on Science Facilities and Equipment (1993) suggests that we might begin our advocacy by helping our boards and school communities recognize the following rationale and philosophy:

Our nation must have a scientifically and technologically literate citizenry that is prepared to understand and deal rationally with the issues and opportunities within a scientific and technological world.

American schools should give science a central role in K–12 instruction where each student should have the opportunity to be engaged in science each day of each school year.

Science and technology occur in many different settings; schools, universities, hospitals, business and industry, as well as government, independent research organizations and scientific organizations. Work places include classrooms, offices, laboratories and natural field settings.

Hands-on laboratory experience is integral to the nature of science and must be included in every science program for every student.

Laboratory experience is critical to the student's cognitive development. Therefore, appropriate facilities must be available and be maintained to support quality science programs.

An Interpretation of the Standards

Evaluating current programs and the facilities that support them is an important part of planning. Does the school district have clearly stated goals and outcomes? Is science an integral part of these goals at all levels? Have the National Science Education Standards impacted these goals and outcomes? Such a review serves both to clarify the direction of the science program and to help to raise the school community's awareness of the importance of the program

In analyzing and developing science programs to meet current needs and remain flexible for future changes, it is useful to consider the following goals suggested by the principles of the Standards:

- The facilities are capable of supporting all of the objectives of the science program.
- Science facilities are available to all students all of the time. At the elementary level, this may mean providing large, self-contained classrooms that have ample access to water; pairing science-friendly classrooms with those that lack the needed resources; or maintaining discovery rooms that provide reasonable access to all teachers when they need them. At the high school level, this means ensuring that enough laboratories are available to enable every student to study a laboratory science every year.
- The facilities and equipment provide a wide selection of experiences appropriate to the learning potential and interests of students with varied capabilities and learning styles. We should continue to seek a deeper understanding of how students at each level learn and to provide facilities that enable us to respond to those needs.
- The science facilities provide laboratory and outdoor space for investigations, demonstrations, and research, including access to natural settings for outdoor science activities.
- The facilities are adaptable. Team teaching, integrated curricular activities, and flexible grouping are well-supported by the physical plant.
- Science classrooms are provided with science supplies, instruments and equipment, and ample, secure space to store these items.
- The arrangement of furniture and utilities in the classroom is flexible so that the teacher is able to direct activities easily while

An elementary science classroom. (4)

Kathe Engster-PA

providing supervision and maintaining maximum control. At the same time, students are able to move around and exit without encountering obstacles.

- Provision is made for easy access to audiovisual resources for individuals and groups under conditions controlled by the classroom teacher.
- Educational technology is within reach, bringing information, data, instrumentation, and research into the classroom, enabling students to explore the world.

The Planning Phase

How do we translate our philosophy, mission, and curriculum into the bricks and mortar of a science learning environment?

Participants

Because the science program and science facilities are so interconnected, the active participation of the teachers, with their extensive experience at the grade level and understanding of the National Science Education Standards and best practice, is crucial to any planning team's success.

There are also many other important participants in the planning process, whether in leadership roles or as valuable sources of input concerning the specific needs of the school, district, curriculum, or program.

For public school projects, members of the school board and the administration usually determine and communicate the community's fiscal constraints and legal requirements and ensure that educational programs and facilities standards are incorporated. Administra-

tors also bring to the team their comprehensive understanding of how the various sectors of the school community interface with each other. Curriculum coordinators present the needs of the program and the requirements of the instruction plans, while community members can contribute essential input into political and family needs. Often, a science supervisor or other science education leader is instrumental in a variety of roles, including coordination, communication, evaluation, and research. Local and state facilities planners and consultants assume various functions and provide important information, perspectives, and ideas. The local facilities planner may coordinate the planning process.

The best planning teams capitalize on the unique characteristics of their communities. Parents and community members should be represented in planning at every step of the way. Business consultants, especially those in science-related corporations, can review equipment and facilities design to determine school-to-work potential; furnishing and equipment consultants will provide specialized advice, while parents may explore opportunities to use the school's facilities for after-school activities. Also useful are the school's custodians and maintenance staff, who are aware of maintenance problems and the value of specific products and can contribute ideas to the design decisions.

Important, but sometimes forgotten, contributors from the school community are the students, whose experiences and opinions should influence decisions regarding space requirements and other aspects of facilities use. Students seldom attend formal meetings,

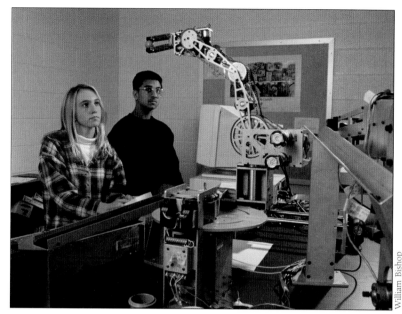

William Bishop

Technology laboratory. (5)

but their input should always be considered.

Whether the project involves remodeling existing space or creating new space, the most important design expert will be the architect, who also provides expertise in engineering, structural requirements, building codes, and safety. If at all possible, it is extremely helpful to include an architectural consultant in the early planning stages. Later, a construction manager or general contractor will also join the team.

Working on a multidisciplinary project team is often a highlight in a teacher's career, but it takes a great deal of time. Teachers are often the team members with the least flexible schedules and most limited time to devote to planning. It helps for other participants to provide the support the teachers need to be able to participate in the process. Schools are encouraged to provide release and/or summer planning time to ensure that faculty input is thorough and not rushed. Finally, curriculum analysis and facility development will require the efforts of many employees, who should be compensated for this invaluable work.

When teachers and curriculum educators assume the major responsibility for planning renovations and new construction, the resulting facilities will be successful in meeting the instructional and developmental needs of the students. Their expertise and experience are the foundation for providing many years of exciting education.

Planning Committee

The planning committee includes a variety of individuals, each with a slightly different perspective on the objectives to be achieved. The committee commonly includes the principal, teachers, science supervisor, superintendent or assistant superintendent, and representative parents and students, and may include other school administrators, science specialists, other instructional specialists, facilities planners, a school board member, an architect, consultants, school support services personnel, and community and business leaders.

The planning committee will usually prepare a statement of needs and may determine educational specifications that provide the basis for decisions on design development. Educational specifications describe the science curriculum and instructional strategy and summarize educational program needs, approximate or specific space needs, and other

information to be used in determining the physical requirements of the facility.

Because of the large number of people usually involved, the planning committee is often grouped into two or more subcommittees.

Curriculum Subcommittee

The curriculum subcommittee should include science teachers from all levels as well as the district's science supervisor and curriculum coordinator. Other potential members are students, parents, a school board member, the assistant superintendent in charge of curriculum, and local business and industry leaders.

The curriculum subcommittee evaluates the school district's entire program, determining how well the sequence of instruction progresses from kindergarten experiences through advanced placement courses in high school, and how this sequence might be modified to accomplish the goals of the National Science Education Standards. It is also charged with ensuring that decisions concerning space, building, landscaping, and other factors meet curriculum requirements. This subcommittee should probably begin its work before the facilities committee gets started, so that the facilities group has some direction with which to evaluate the existing facilities.

Facilities Subcommittee

The facilities subcommittee includes the district's facilities administrator, the science supervisor or coordinator, one or more science teachers, and, if possible, an architect with experience in school science facilities. It may also include students, parents, a science facilities consultant, and a school board member.

Furniture and equipment consultants and suppliers, business and industry representatives, and other community leaders may also participate.

This subcommittee's responsibility is to evaluate any existing science facilities with respect to the curriculum guidelines established by the curriculum subcommittee, and to analyze the physical needs of the district's science program based on the anticipated curriculum, enrollment, and other factors.

Project Oversight

One way to make the review process more efficient, in some circumstances, is to select a small decision-making team whose job it is to keep the others up to date and receive their input, but who have the power to make decisions. Such a project oversight committee might, for example, have three voting members, who follow the project from beginning to end and work directly with the architect and construction manager or a general contractor. The school principal, superintendent, representative parents, and a few other key figures can be included in regular meetings with the architect and later with the construction team, but the decision-making responsibility in such cases rests with the three representative voting members. This can eliminate the need for much of the large-group consensus work.

The Planning Process

The planning committee, in consultation with the superintendent, school board, and other participants, must consider every aspect of project development, ranging from the nature of the science program to budgetary constraints. It also includes such factors as the number and nature of science facilities needed, clustering facilities, safety requirements, technology needs, adaptations for students with disabilities, government regulations, and maintenance requirements.

The usual sequence and approximate timing of the various steps and stages of planning and construction are expressed graphically in sample time lines later in the text. These include the following:
- define the science curriculum
- evaluate the existing facilities
- "program" the science space needs
- review and approve the program
- present to the board of education
- obtain financing
- select the architect
- develop and approve the schematic design
- develop and approve the final design
- solicit and evaluate bids
- construction
- specify, fabricate, and install the furnishings and equipment
- move in

Defining the Science Curriculum

The first major step in the planning process is curriculum review. The curriculum subcommittee evaluates the school district's science program to ensure that the curriculum has been defined. In some cases, a standing or special committee will devote months to developing the curriculum. To make certain that facilities will not become outdated quickly, the staff should have opportunities to review current trends and directions in curriculum and instruction.

Later, periodic mid-design review meetings will ensure that this valuable input from the faculty is not lost as the project develops.

Planners should consider consulting with teachers of pre-kindergarten, extended day, fifth-year high school, and other special programs. Even though the science team is not responsible for the curriculum for these programs, the committee can provide a service by designing spaces that are science-friendly.

Evaluating Existing Facilities

An inventory of current facilities can be a powerful tool for advocacy in the early stages of planning. It is often useful for the science supervisor, teachers, administrators, and perhaps the facilities director or other interested participants to conduct an early walk-through of a school's facilities for a preliminary quick assessment, using a checklist as a guide. The resulting, relatively brief, inventory may be used to help alert administrators, parent groups, and the school board to the school's greatest needs as part of the larger needs assessment process.

An architectural consultant and members of the facilities subcommittee should conduct a more extensive and detailed evaluation later, to use in preparing materials to be presented to the school board.

The three sample checklists in Appendix E may be expanded and adapted to reflect the needs and goals of individual schools and programs. The items are not meant to be complete or exhaustive. Appropriate guidelines may be selected using the detailed suggestions and recommendations found throughout this book. Consult Chapter 3 for information on questions of safety and accessibility, and Chapters 4 through 6 for most other topics. See also the safety survey in Appendix B.

Determining the Nature of the Facilities

"Programming" is the initial step in developing a plan for the physical facilities. Its purpose is to determine what types of spaces the science program will require, how many of each type of space are needed, how the spaces should relate to each other, and what special needs each space will have, including dimensions. These decisions are made in response to the science program's instructional and educational requirements.

To estimate the amount of space needed, planners should imagine the most generous amount of laboratory space available for each student today and multiply that by the number of students expected in the laboratory in the future. The trend is toward an increasing need for more space to conduct safe and effective science programs.

In order to predict future science enrollment, planners should consider the projected growth in the school population, changes in demographics, neighboring feeder schools, and other factors such as local business growth.

The National Science Teachers Association recommends a maximum class size of 24 students in elementary and middle school science classes and high school laboratories.

Category	Guidelines
Is there adequate floor space for the students to work safely?	40 sq. ft min. per student for science room; 45 sq. ft min. for multiple-use classroom; Sufficient space between desks; 4-ft aisles
Is there adequate space for the teachers?	Secure storage and desks; Space available to teacher during planning time
Is the power supply adequate and safe?	Ground-fault interrupters; Separate circuits for computers; No loose wires with pull-down cords or power poles
Is the lighting adequate?	Bright, not yellow, diffused to avoid glare; 50 foot-candles, min., per sq. ft; 75–100 foot-candles at the work surface
Is there safe and adequate storage?	Secure storage; 10 sq. ft per student for storage and preparation space; No sharp corners; Adequate space for lab and AV equipment
Is there a good infrastructure for communications?	Telephone for emergencies; Networking wiring for computers; Cable for video communication; Television or LCD projector; Room-darkening shades or blinds
Are there counters or tables for investigations?	Counters 36" high for adults, 24" high for grades 3-5; 27" high for grades 3-5; Tables 18-20" high for grades K-2, 21-23" high for grades 3-5

Clustering Facilities

The desired relationship between the science facilities and all other school areas should be determined early in the planning process. In middle and high school, for example, this might include providing easy access to the media center, technology education area, or computer center, or to the home economics, agricultural science, fine arts, or graphics rooms. Since science facilities are very costly, providing access to and from applied science areas can help ease the budget and contribute to students' understanding of the interrelationship of disciplines.

The location of science facilities within a school has an important impact on how well the science program works. If the science discovery center is far from the general education classroom, time will be lost during class changes and the facility will be used less frequently. If the location of a facility is essential to the program, this element should be built into the planning process. In many elementary schools, locating the science center adjacent to the art, music, or physical education rooms should be considered. Traffic patterns along the halls leading to these rooms and the noise generated by students and equipment are additional factors to be analyzed.

In middle and high school, the relative locations of the science classrooms are also important planning issues. Should the biology classroom be next to the chemistry room? In some large high schools, the division of the school population into semiautonomous houses or pods may result in decentralized science facilities. However, isolating physics or advanced biochemistry laboratories may be counterproductive to the curricular objectives of the department.

Planning for Future Change

For teachers, participating in a design team is both a challenge and an opportunity, as it requires them to consider what they really want

Figure 1.

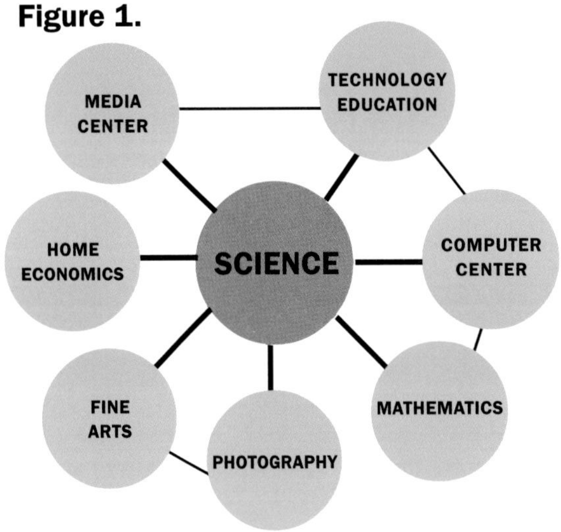

Recommended adjacencies.

to accomplish educationally and to decide what types of physical facilities will enable them to reach their objectives. However, teachers must also bear in mind that they will not be the only instructors to use the facilities they are planning. Because most classrooms outlive the careers of those they first serve, teachers must think about the science teaching of the future and how to design space today that will serve their successors for decades.

For example, in the seventies, many schools were built around an "open classroom" concept, with teaching stations clustered around a media area without complete walls to separate the stations. By the next decade, schools were rebuilding enclosed classrooms as teachers moved "back to basics" and wanted private spaces. In the eighties, the movement toward integrated curricula caused schools to begin incorporating more science-friendly equipment into all classrooms. What will the future bring?

Obtaining Approval and Financing

Once the programming has been completed and the result reviewed by the planning committee and approved by the board of education, the remaining steps involve funding, architectural design, construction, furnishing, and, finally, occupancy.

The process for getting legal approval for major construction projects varies from state to state. While a small renovation may be accomplished by a simple vote of a board of education, most construction work will require public votes and the issuance of bonds.

Thus, advocacy does not end with the planning process. To achieve community approval of the request for new school construction, planners use their expertise and the experience of others, networking with the staff of newly constructed schools in similar communities with the help of the team's architect or construction manager. Accurate and consistent estimates of the total cost of the project should be made available in order to maintain the public's confidence.

Selecting the Architect

After the financing has been approved, the school team selects the architect who will create the design and administer the construction contract. If planning funds are available to compensate the architect, the design phase may begin earlier and proceed in parallel with the financing process. In some cases, the architect will have been working with the planning team from the beginning.

While architectural training promotes understanding of construction methods and human needs, architects differ widely in their style and sensitivity to student issues. Careful interviews and visits to the architect's previous projects are vital—and planners should not forget to interview the teachers who work in these facilities.

The Design Phase

The architect will address the educational needs when designing the facility to meet the objectives of the planning committee.

The architectural design phase can take as little as three months for a simple renovation to six or eight months for a large addition. It begins with the creation of a schematic design and concludes with the final design documents that serve as building instructions for the contractor.

A laboratory/classroom, from a supplier's catalog. (6)

Fisher Hamilton

Professional laboratory consultants and many other experts can contribute to the design team. Equipment consultants and suppliers are happy to provide information. The fire marshal or state fire inspector is a frequent source of advice, either on site or via off-site review. Civil engineers for soil and foundation work, mechanical engineers for heating and plumbing systems, and electrical engineers for power and technology, will each be essential to some aspects of the project. Building inspectors and historic preservation commissions may make contributions, and interior designers can add to the appearance of a project and the quality of the learning environment.

The construction phase of the project and various construction-related topics, including the budget, are discussed later in this chapter.

The Role of the Science Education Leader

We shape our facilities and afterwards our facilities shape us.
—Paraphrasing Sir Winston Churchill

The science supervisor, science coordinator, or other science education leader plays a key role in the design, planning, and development of science facilities. The leader ensures that the design will create learning environments that support curricular improvements, appropriate assessment, educational change, excellence, and equity. The science education leader's work starts long before the planning stage, because of the amount of information that will be required.

A major task for the science education leader is to make sure that curriculum improvement drives the design process. He or she serves on or chairs the curriculum subcommittee and functions as the curriculum consultant on the planning team.

In this role, the science education leader must be prepared to answer the following questions:

- What science curriculum will the students be following?
- How might this curriculum change in the future?
- What curricular improvements must be supported by the new facilities?
- What types of facilities and equipment will

be needed to implement these curricular improvements and facilitate learning activities?

- Will the proposed design of the facilities help to implement the curricular improvements?

One important objective is to support the recommended designs and equipment by

- presenting research evidence that they have been used effectively
- describing how they will be used to enhance and improve the curriculum, instruction, and assessment, and why alternative options will not
- explaining how they will resolve difficulties in teaching and learning science
- building confidence by showing how they agree with national and local standards and by obtaining the teachers' support

Supervisory Roles

The various functions the science education leader performs in the course of assisting the planning team in its mission include the following.

Planning and coordination. The science education leader plans needs assessments and workflow analyses, organizes tours of exemplary science facilities, facilitates meetings between teachers and administrators, and may serve as the liaison between instructional staff and architects.

Information and communication. The science education leader tracks and disseminates information on innovations and anticipated trends in curriculum and instruction. This includes

- identifying guidelines and expectations for improving the facilities
- supplying the planning team with model floor plans, room designs, and equipment lists
- describing specific requirements for casework, furniture, and equipment
- informing administrators and teaching staff about specifications for the facilities.

Evaluation. The science education leader reviews architectural plans, specifications, and drawings for the facilities to strengthen instructional options; analyzes, updates, and issues safety requirements in compliance with state standards and accepted educational practices; and plans the safe use of chemicals, electric power, biological materials, equipment, and safety devices.

Promotion and representation. The science education leader participates in fundraising for the facilities project and for promoting educational improvements. Other duties include representing the planning committee at educational events at schools, science centers, PTA and community meetings, professional development workshops, and local and national education meetings.

Addressing the School Board

Although school board systems differ significantly across the country, in almost every state, the first step to getting approval for renovating or building a science facility is winning the approval of the board of education. In 40 states, the approval process for major construction projects begins when voters endorse the board's request for a bond issue or an increase in the millage. In other states, a simple majority vote of the board can provide the capital to construct new facilities. Learning how the board operates and how to communicate with it are essential skills, and presenting an effective case for a facilities project may be the defining moment in the concept's progress toward realization.

Usually, the planning committee prepares the case, which is reviewed by the superintendent before the superintendent or assistant superintendent, the science education leader, or a teacher presents it to the board.

Communicating with the Board

All communications with the board should be coordinated through the superintendent or his or her designee. Because most board members serve part time, they rely heavily on the information gathered by the administrative staff and presented to them by the superintendent. As a result, the relationship between the board and the superintendent is crucial, as is the superintendent's support of the proposed project.

Communication with board members is best done through the appropriate channels and chain of command, rather than through informal conversations with individual members. A phone call or conversation with a board member may be counterproductive if it catches the superintendent off guard. Similarly, working with a single member can backfire, as the best boards prefer to work through committees to reach consensus.

The Presentation

The most successful presentations are those that acknowledge the board members' point of view. Members must weigh their desire for academic excellence against their responsibility for fiscal restraint. The clear majority must be able to see the cost effectiveness of the proposal and be confident that they can communicate the program's value to their constituents.

Important questions to address in a presentation to a board include:

Why should we approve the project?

What evidence is there that the project will be successful?

How will students benefit?

How many students will benefit?

How will the project promote equity?

How long will it take to complete the project?

Is the project cost effective?

Will the project have lasting value?

The proposal should be compatible with the district's mission statement and strategic plan, and its ideas consistent with the long-range thrust of these policies. It helps to show that all possible alternatives have already been explored and to cite similar projects that have been successful. Data from educational sources will support an explanation of what the facilities will need to meet the objectives of the National Science Education Standards and conform to the requirements of the construction industry.

When it is time to address the board, the presenter should work with the superintendent to plan the time and format of the presentation, which will most likely be at a public meeting. The speaker should address the board through its president (Mr. or Madam President), refer to colleagues and administrators by their formal names, and, finally, re-member to thank the board for its time.

Building the Science Facility

Charting the Path

How long will it take to renovate the science facility or build a new one? The answer is, usually much longer than we think, given the requirements of obtaining approval and financing, the detailed planning and competitive bidding that precede all public works, and a variety of possible unknowns and delays of construction.

Attention to scheduling and communication is critical to the success of the project. Even the wisest purchases and most skilled contractor cannot compensate for the havoc that inadequate project coordination can cause. The facilities planner or another coordinator should consult with the members of the planning team and make sure that all parties are using the same software.

Time Line

The two sample time lines shown—one for a renovation and one for new construction, such as a science wing—indicate some of the basic steps involved in the planning, designing, and construction phases of a project.

Each of these examples illustrates one way the steps might fit together in a particular context and given a particular set of factors. In practice, the sequencing of many of the steps will vary considerably in different situations, as will the time required for each step.

The architect may be selected before or af-ter the bonding or financing process, depending on the circumstances. In fact, an architect often works with the planning committee from the beginning and may be chosen for the design contract as well.

Construction

Construction will be the responsibility of either a construction manager (CM) or a general contractor (GC). Many school districts have facilities planners who are responsible for communicating with the architect. Otherwise, the architect will be the primary communicator between the planning team and the construction team and be charged with seeing that the philosophy and requirements defined by the team become a reality. It is important that the team make its wishes and needs known to the architect.

Usually, a general contractor will be selected to manage new construction, where the variables are fairly well known, while a construction management firm may be used to handle renovations where unexpected factors are more likely to arise.

Construction managers conduct on-site supervision of projects for a set fee; they have extensive expertise with codes, estimating, budgeting, and labor regulations. When a school employs a CM, the contracts for electrical work, mechanical work, masonry, etc. are issued by the school district and sequenced and supervised by the construction manager. The use of construction management firms in renovations and school projects has been increasing.

A general contractor is usually selected through an all-inclusive, lump-sum, competi-

Figure 2.

Example of a Time Line for New Construction
(Durations Shown in Months)

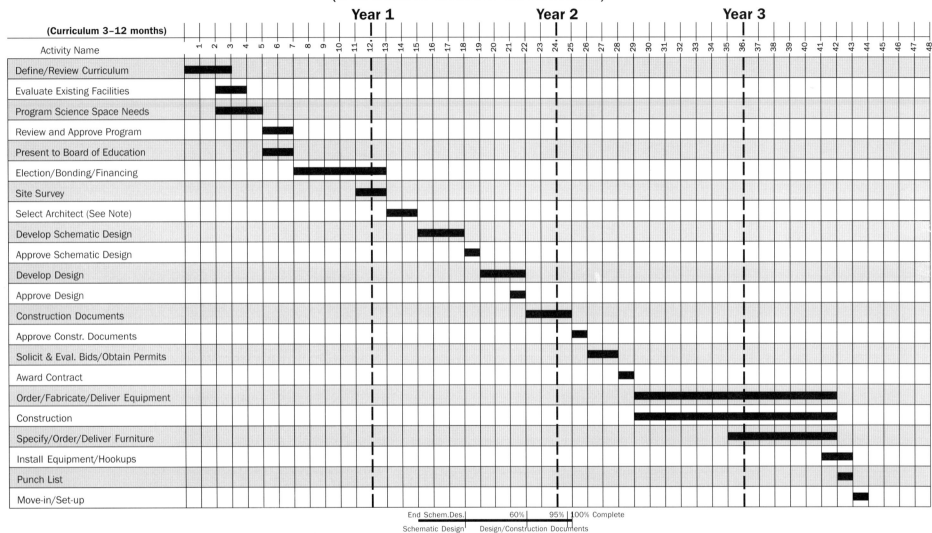

Notes:

1. Curriculum development may take up to 12 months; a review, approximately 3 months.
2. Evaluation of existing facilities includes reviewing the hazardous materials survey.
3. Timing and length of the bonding/financing process vary considerably.
4. The architect may be selected at the start (if funds are available) or at the end of the bonding process. An architectural consultant often works with the planning team from the beginning.
5. Cost estimates are calculated when the schematic design is completed and again when the construction documents are 60% and 95% complete.
6. Movable equipment (including furniture) is sometimes purchased separately from the construction contract. Some items must be ordered early, and items such as computers should be ordered as late as possible.
7. Construction time includes routine delays due to weather.
8. It is usual to build a contingency into the schedule for unexpected delays.
9. A punch list, made by the architect or the contractor, shows incomplete or faulty work.
10. The warranty period may continue for up to 12 months after occupancy.

Figure 3.

Example of a Time Line for a Renovation
(Durations Shown in Weeks)

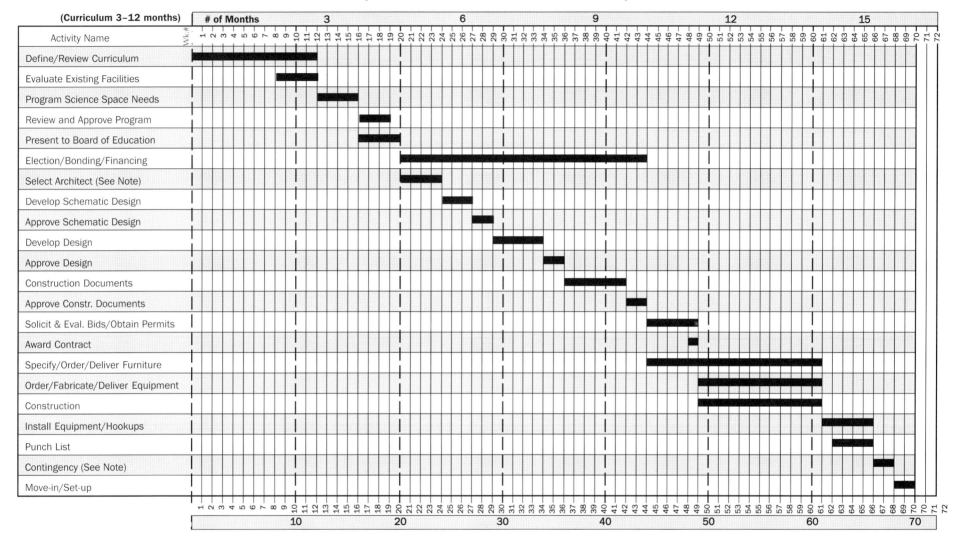

Notes:

1. In this example, funds are available to select the architect at the start of the bonding process.
2. Fixed equipment, which includes science lab casework and lab tables, is normally part of the construction contract.
3. If a renovation is planned for the summer months, bidding for equipment must be conducted early to ensure timely delivery. The architect and owner may choose to solicit bids early for the casework.
4. Furniture and other movable equipment are purchased separately from the construction contract.
5. The contingency time allowance helps compensate for unexpected delays throughout the project.

A Budget for a High School Addition

Building Construction Cost		
(10,000 square feet x $109/square foot)		$1,090,000.00
Site Development Costs		100,000.00
Off-Site Construction Costs		75,000.00
Landscaping		10,000.00
Movable Equipment		150,000.00
	Subtotal	$1,425,000.00
Design Contingency (10% of Subtotal)		142,500.00
Construction Contingency (5% of Subtotal)		71,250.00
Architect and Engineer Fees (7% of Subtotal)		99,750.00
Surveying		1,500.00
Geotechnical Investigations		3,500.00
Building Permit		5,500.00
Owner Miscellaneous Cost Allowance		10,000.00
Data Network Wiring Allowance		30,000.00
Furniture		200,000.00
	Subtotal	$1,989,000.00
Inflation (3% x Subtotal)		59,670.00
	Total Building Costs	$2,048,670.00

tive bidding process. The GC assumes responsibility for completing the construction, supervising all phases of the work, and issuing all of the subcontracts to trade contractors.

Paying the Bill

At all stages of the planning process, every step must be budget conscious. Whether the project is a small one financed by an endowment or general operating funds, or a major

effort financed by the sale of municipal bonds, the scope of the work to be undertaken must always be determined with the advice of experts on the funds available.

To planners whose usual responsibilities do not include such major expenditures, the cost of construction can be numbing. The work done for public entities involves the services of registered architects and engineers, a variety of technical consultants, and contractors or construction managers—whose combined fees can add between 15 and 20 percent to the cost of construction.

When schools must raise a bond by public referendum to finance construction, the process of determining how much a project will cost can be complex. The district can seldom afford to do complete designs and estimates before the project is approved. So the school team must go to the voters with only an estimated value for a partially designed plan. After the voters give their approval, the team completes the planning process, adhering to the strict financial limits imposed by the public.

Developing a Project Budget

The following example illustrates the types of costs that should be considered in determining an overall project budget, and of their relative magnitudes. The costs of this project are taken from a real example. Of course, the budget for any project must be individually developed, because construction costs, fees, and scope vary widely from project to project, from one location to another, and at different times.

In this example, a high school science addition of 10,000 square feet is being constructed with an overall project duration of

two years, from the beginning of planning and design, not counting curriculum review, to final occupancy. The base construction cost per square foot was taken from *Means Building Construction Cost Data 1999*, for a 3/4 cost-level (the book's term for higher-end cost) high school. A design/bid/build approach was used, without a construction manager.

Note that these are not the only costs associated with a project. This budget doesn't include the costs of the purchase of land or costs related to a bond election and payment of interest. In renovations, any costs of hazardous material abatement such as asbestos or lead-based paint must be added, as these are generally not included in the construction costs and fees.

In a budget,

- the construction cost is generally an estimate of the general contractor's bid for the building.
- site development costs include such items as grading, roads, and retaining walls.
- off-site construction is the construction that needs to be done on the property of others, such as extending water lines, sewers, and roads to the site.
- landscaping includes new trees, shrubs, and other plantings.
- movable equipment includes large items such as movable laboratory tables and carts.
- the contingencies are figures to cover unpredictable costs.
- the costs of most engineering consultants are generally included in the architect's fee.
- surveying, generally required for a new building, and geotechnical investigations

to evaluate soil conditions are usually contracted for by the owner.

- data network wiring is often performed by a separate contractor.
- furniture is often purchased separately from the construction contract and includes design and specification costs.
- inflation is considered, because the construction market will probably change by the time bids are taken; the effects of inflation average out to one half the annual rate of inflation over the construction period. Here, it is calculated as one half of 3 percent over two years, or .015 x 2 x the final subtotal.

Relocation

When doing a renovation, it is important to determine and plan for the financial consequences of any "swing time"—moving into temporary quarters—as well as the disruptions to the school.

Limiting the construction period to the summer vacation may greatly increase the cost of a job, due to overtime charges and, often, because construction contractors may be busier in the summer. It is worth finding out whether it would be possible to have the work continue during the school year. Can fences, barriers, and temporary relocations make construction safe? Other factors to consider are noise, odors, dust, blocked access, and strangers in the building. This situation requires careful analysis. For any project that is estimated to last longer than two months, very serious consideration must be given to vacating the construction area. The extent of hazards and disruptions caused by coexisting with construction are rarely well understood until they have been experienced.

Controlling Extra Costs

It helps for planners to acquire a background in some of the mysteries of the construction process, such as pricing and collecting competitive bids. In almost all public construction, the contractors are chosen by a closed, competitive bidding process after the design has been completed.

One budget category is *general conditions*. The fence that separates the project from the school, copying plans, express deliveries, builders' cellular phones, and even the portable toilets are general conditions items. They are not formally part of the job, but the job will not get done without them.

There are ways to keep change orders to a reasonable level. For example, an appointed representative from the district might be authorized to approve every change order up to a certain limit as long as the total does not exceed the budgeted contingency; this person must have a clear understanding of those estimates, expressed in dollars, that will need formal action by the board.

Another budget item that may be unfamiliar to the planning team is the contingency fund. This is a figure, amounting to between 10 and 15 percent of the estimated total cost, that is added to the budget to cover unforeseen events. The percentage for the contingency figure for a renovation project should be higher than for new construction, because of the greater potential for hidden adverse conditions. In renovation projects, the builders often find surprises behind the walls, and even the best-drawn plans will require changes. In new construction projects, unforeseen problems with the condition of the soil can require corrective measures. In these cases, the builder will seek authorization to add charges to the original estimate. These are some of the reasons why it is almost unheard of for the final bill to be the same as the original quoted price.

A good architect designs within budget limits and communicates with the planning team to set priorities. At the same time,

A typical building site for new science facilities. (7)

Figure 4.

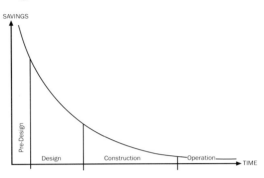

Value engineering can produce greater savings if it is performed early in the planning and design of a project.

Adapted from *Value Engineering in the Construction Industry* (p. 2), by Alphonse Dell'Isola, Construction Publishing Co., New York, 1974.

Figure 5.

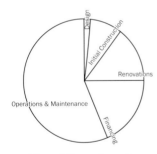

The relative values of the various life-cycle costs of a building.

a professional estimator from the architectural or construction management firm can keep track of market conditions and make good estimates of construction costs. But even with all of this professional help, it is the planning team that must manage the budget—while bearing in mind that initial construction costs, life-cycle costs of maintenance and operations, and aesthetics are important factors. If cuts must be made, the educators must make the calls. Deciding between two desirable features is often a task best left to people with classroom experience.

One or two cost estimates should be performed early in the design process, before the final documents have progressed to a point where making changes is time consuming and costly. Usually, these would be performed at the completion of the schematic design and at the 60 percent document review stage.

If an estimate suggests that a project is over budget, the architects and their consultants should engage in *value engineering*, the process whereby a list of alternative ways to achieve the same design goals within the budget is prepared and evaluated. These alternatives may include making changes in the brands of materials or equipment, simplifying design elements, or even making small alterations in the drawings to change the sequence of the installation of materials. This process increases the chance that bids will come in within the budget. Sometimes, merely changing the mix and timing of tasks can make the difference. For example, a contractor who has to wait while other skilled craftsmen do a small job will add the cost of that time to the bid.

The value engineering concept has been adopted by architects and construction managers in an effort to stretch the value of a construction dollar. It can produce greater savings if it is performed early in the planning and design of a project, when the time and cost implications of making a change are lowest. The longer one waits, the higher the cost of making the change and the lower the resulting life-cycle cost changes. Waiting until the bids are in before seeking less expensive ways of constructing the building indicates that the design and construction team has not been completely effective during the planning and design stages. Suggested changes after bids are received are more likely to reduce the quality of the project, and the value as well.

Throughout the budgeting process, the key concept is prioritization. The overall goals of the project must be kept at the forefront. It does not hurt to post them in the meeting room, to remind everyone to stay on target. When the facilities are completed, the weeks and months of decision-making and work will be rewarded with a positive result.

References

Dell'Isola, Alphonse J. (1974). *Value Engineering in the Construction Industry*. New York: Construction Publishing Co.

Means Building Construction Cost Data 1999 (54th ed.). (1998). Kingston, MA: R.S. Means.

National Science Teachers Association Task Force on Science Facilities and Equipment. (1993). *Facilitating Science Facilities: A Priority*. Arlington, VA: National Science Teachers Association.

CHAPTER 2

Current Trends and Future Directions in Science Education

Conducting scientific inquiry requires that students have easy, equitable, and frequent opportunities to use a wide range of equipment, materials, supplies, and other resources for experimentation and direct investigation of phenomena.

—National Science Education Standards, p. 220

One of the most exciting aspects of the planning process is the opportunity to plan for the future. Foresight in planning can expand the potential of science learning environments for decades to come. This brief outline is intended as a summary of some of the changes that are occurring in science education. To understand the likely extent of these changes and their implications for school facilities design, attention to the Standards and a review of relevant research are recommended.

Standards-Based Programs

The simplest educational concept—and perhaps the most significant—to consider in designing tomorrow's science programs is inquiry. In keeping with the Standards' strong emphasis on inquiry-based programs, students increasingly will be exploring the world inside and outside the classroom. The move toward inquiry will mean that more space and greater flexibility will be needed in science facilities. There will also be a need for more extensive storage space because of the increased need for equipment and the greater emphasis on student projects.

Many other trends and changes, including some that are discussed below, are likely to be sustained because of the support given in the Standards.

Integrated Curricula

Science no longer stands alone, especially in kindergarten through grade 8. While many elementary schools are still building specialized science or discovery rooms, the trend toward teaching science every day and linking it to social studies, mathematics, and language arts has created pressure to make every classroom science-friendly. Where this is not possible due to space limitations, some schools have paired versatile multiple-use classrooms with classrooms geared to language arts in order to encourage sharing of the facilities and thereby make space for running investigations available to all students

A major issue in elementary science education is whether the greater portion of the program will be taught by the general education teacher or by a specialist. If it is to be the

Going on a field trip. (8)

classroom teacher, who will help manage shared supplies and equipment? Or will supplies and equipment be duplicated in each classroom? This is an example of how curricular issues can affect the use of facilities, with decisions varying in different communities. The solution lies in building facilities that have great flexibility.

Many middle schools have been moving from departmentalized programs, with all laboratories taken together, to an interdisciplinary teaming approach, with one science teacher for each team, creating problems where current facilities do not allow easy access for each cluster of students. Similarly, some large high schools are also dividing their student bodies into smaller "houses."

Finally, as science curricula in middle school and high school become more integrated, increased space and flexibility of facilities, as well as the relative locations of the classrooms, become more important.

Co-Teaching and Inclusion

Students who are challenged or at risk are seldom separated from the general education classrooms, and special-needs teachers usually work in the general education environment. This situation demands more space and more flexible classroom arrangements for small-group work. Regulations require wider aisles and other adjustments and modifications for students with disabilities.

Some disabled students need intensive, separate assistance at certain times, such as during the administration of a test. The ease of access by these students to a resource room is also a factor for the planning team to consider. Excluding science students with disabilities from authentic laboratory facilities is unthinkable, and a violation of state and federal laws.

Independent Projects

Tomorrow's students will have more opportunities to follow their own curiosity. Independent projects require extensive space for work and for storage. Because of the constraints of liability law, teachers need to have constant access to those students who are working independently. This may mean providing separate glassed-in space or other means of supervision, so that teachers can manage several spaces at the same time. In early elementary classes, overhead mirrors and appropriately sized room dividers create spaces for independent exploration without compromising accessibility or supervision.

Secondary Courses

Although secondary courses change slowly, they are taking on a different appearance as we move toward the future, creating the need for more space for laboratories and storage. The most important change relevant to facility needs is that more students are studying science, partly because the requirement that high school students take a minimum of three years of laboratory science is becoming more common.

Biology and Earth science courses are changing dramatically, with both including more chemistry and investigations than ever before. The movement toward integrated courses at the middle and high school levels has already been mentioned.

Finally, there is increased demand for programs, such as applied physics, that have become more popular with students because of

the integration of industrial model equipment into the programs.

Instructional Methods

Perhaps the most difficult aspect of facility planning is accommodating individual instructional styles, especially at the secondary level. Despite the trends toward more active student participation and increased cooperative work, many teachers still prefer lecture-style instruction, and most instructional models include at least a short, 20-minute, period for a lecture. Should the new science rooms accommodate lecture-style seating arrangements?

Some of today's teachers prefer the sound-absorbing characteristics of cinder block walls, while others prefer the folding walls that allow team teaching. Can and should both be accommodated? Some expensive post-construction remodeling has been undertaken in the past when teachers discovered that they could not function in some open classrooms or other non-traditional facilities that well-meaning planning teams had designed for them.

While there is not necessarily a set answer to issues raised in response to instructional preferences, two guiding principles are useful. First, make a firm commitment to adapt the facilities to the Standards' recommendations. Change may be slow, but it is coming, and most construction projects are built for decades of use. Secondly, do not expect the new facilities to result in a change in methodology overnight. While they present an appropriate environment for newly trained teachers and can remove barriers for teachers who want to change, they will not motivate those who have little inclination to do so.

Technology and Tomorrow's Curriculum

No paper publication could hope to keep pace with the cutting edge of school technology. Nevertheless, the trends and implications of technology in school programs are major considerations for every planning team. The keys to ensuring that learning spaces will not become outmoded quickly are a good understanding of the general direction of the changes to come and a commitment to flexibility in everything that is installed.

The essential element in school technology is communication. The global village may be a cliche, but the global classroom is a reality. New facilities should be designed with multiple access sites to the Internet and the world. Phones for voice communication, cable for video and data, and computers for data processing, are all essential. Although the newest communication access systems combine phone, voice, and data in a single cable, the most important part of the communication system is still the basic equipment used for accessing telephone lines. Today's project teams do not debate whether to put a computer in the classroom or in the laboratory: both rooms require them.

A second element is flexibility. When the budget is tight, adequate wiring should be installed in the walls during the construction stage and the plans should include fiber and cable wiring accessible from almost everywhere. This will save money by allowing the installation of additional lines in the future.

Planning to address the need for computers in the classroom means creating a comprehensive list that includes processing speeds, amount of memory, hardware, software, delivery times, installation, and service.

In addition to computers, scientific instruments and many other kinds of technological equipment are also needed in the science classroom. In addition, wide counters equipped with separate circuits for power are necessary to accommodate the equipment. Easy access to shared equipment, such as copiers, is also necessary.

In just a few months during 1997, the delivery of state-of-the-art video moved from cable to digital data videostreaming. Every year, the capacity of processors to access data doubles. The task of the planning committee becomes harder when it is realized that the state of the art may change from the time of the groundbreaking ceremony to the dedication of the facility! Whether the planning committee is able to achieve its goals easily or faces difficult choices, it is imperative to make decisions that will not preclude the adoption of current and future advancements.

Distance Learning

Perhaps because of facility limitations, the buzzword of the late nineties, "distance learning," has not lived up to expectations, but the need to provide links in the classroom is still essential in most new school construction.

The process is best suited for foreign languages and higher-level specialty classes that consist primarily of lectures, discussions, and problem solving and attract small enrollments. Distance learning is invaluable for rural schools that need access to instructional or disciplinary expertise. Finally, the facilities have proved valuable for clubs and professional meetings. Efforts to package science coursework for delivery through one-way distance learning have been far less successful. A prepackaged physics course for a remote school may be better than nothing at all, but according to many experts, not by much.

Normally, distance learning at its best means interactive audio/video/voice access between two or more classrooms. Three video cameras are needed. Small classrooms—for classes of under 20 students—are usually the norm, for good visibility and communication. Because of the expense of the equipment, a distance learning facility will probably not be used for many school functions other than video production, so it should be seen as a specialized facility. If students are to access the facility without full-time supervision, it is practical to locate the facility next to the media center or technology pod.

CHAPTER 3

Safety, Accessibility, and Legal Guidelines

There has been a long history of tort litigation involving safety in school facilities. Interestingly, the first line of defense for districts, school boards, employees, architects, and contractors, which is to build safe facilities and purchase appropriate furniture and equipment, also fosters excellence in science instruction. Proper facilities provide safe environments for science education and minimize litigation.

Building for Safety

School laboratory design can support safety in many ways, such as providing ample work space, facilitating the supervision of students, incorporating safety features, and avoiding hazards. Planners will need to investigate the variety of federal regulations and local and state codes and standards that apply. These can have a significant impact on design decisions. Information is available from school district officials, local government building officials, state and local fire marshals, and the relevant federal agencies.

Adequate Space

The most important factor in designing school safety is space. Providing adequate space is common sense, and research has found that it reduces accidents. A significant increase in

accidents occurs when the floor space per student in a laboratory is less than 41 square feet at the high school level (Young, 1972). A minimum of 45 square feet per student for a laboratory is recommended. A minimum of 60 square feet per student is needed for a combination laboratory/classroom, given current teaching practices.

The use of technology in the classroom and requirements of compliance with the Americans with Disabilities Act (ADA) and Individuals with Disabilities in Education Act (IDEA) have increased the amount of space required for a safe classroom environment.

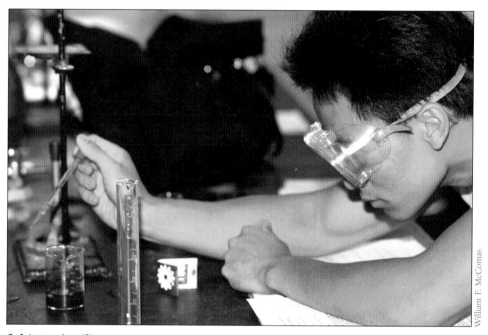

Safety goggles. (9)

William F. McComas

In addition to the floor space allotted per student, approximately 20 square feet is needed to comply with ADA guidelines for an adapted student workstation. Fifteen square feet is required for each computer station, as well as space for other technological equipment. Changes in science programs and instructional methods have also resulted in a need for increased classroom and support space.

The square footage needed for a laboratory,

science classroom, or combination classroom/laboratory depends on the number of students in the room. The NSTA 1990 Position Statement on Laboratory Science recommends that the number of students assigned to each class in elementary school and middle school and to each laboratory class in high school be no more than 24. Although class size should never exceed this figure, even with adequate space, it is wise for planners to make allow-

Minimum Recommended Floor Space per Student, in Square Feet

	Elementary School	Middle School	High School
Science Room	40		
Multiple-Use Classroom	45		
Pure Laboratory		45	45
Combination Lab./Classroom		60	60

Minimum Room Size for a Class of 24, in Square Feet

	Elementary School	Middle School	High School
Science Room	960		
Multiple-Use Classroom	1,080		
Pure Laboratory		1,080	1,080
Combination Lab./Classroom		1,440	1,440

ance for future classes that may be slightly larger than today's.

Laboratories should be built to accommodate the number of students likely to be assigned to them. Crowded classrooms cause students to work too closely together, preventing them from escaping from hazards and hampering teachers' ability to circulate and supervise students. Besides adequate floor space, students need their own work areas, with ample work surfaces and a sufficient number of shared sinks and heat sources, in order to work safely.

Emergency Exits

Another crucial concern is the ability to exit safely from classrooms during emergencies. Students of all ages and adults must be able to find their way out of a school in a prompt and orderly manner. It is advisable that school buildings with over 20,000 square feet of floor space have at least two exits from every classroom, with one leading to the outside. For any building, two or more exits are recommended for every laboratory and preparation room. These should be at opposite ends of the room, with doors opening outward.

The National Fire Protection Association (NFPA) 1997, Life Safety Code requires a minimum of two exit access doorways in most laboratories that are greater than 1,000 square feet. Local and state fire regulations apply.

Electricity

Electrical safety needs must be considered from the beginning of the design process. Ground-fault interrupters (GFI) protect people against major shock and electrical fires by pre-

venting short circuits, and should be installed on all outlets in the laboratory. Even with this protection, outlets should not be close to sinks or other water sources. All outlets in the school must be grounded, as required under Occupational Safety and Health Act (OSHA) regulations, to prevent electrical accidents. Surge protectors are used to protect computers and other electronic devices from power surges, which may be random or induced by lightning.

Sufficient electrical outlets should be provided to avoid the need for extension cords, which present safety hazards. When considering alternatives to wall outlets, it is important to investigate their pros and cons with respect to safety. Floor boxes should never be located close to water sources or areas where water is used.

Emergency shut-off controls for electrical service should be available to the teacher, but not easily accessible to the students. They are normally located near the teacher's station and not far from the door. DC lines should not be used.

Only spark-free refrigeration should be used in laboratories, preparation rooms, and storage rooms, for storage of flammables or protection from inadvertent exposure to flammables.

Gas

All sources of heat present potential safety problems. The decision to use gas or alternative heat sources in laboratories depends on instructional and preparation needs, and the procedures for minimizing hazards.

The control valve for shutting off the gas in

the laboratory when the teacher is not present or when lessons do not require gas should be accessible only to the teacher. If a preparation room has shutoffs for several classrooms, these must be clearly labeled to indicate which lines they control.

The room should have an emergency shut-off valve activated by pushing a highly visible button, with a keyed reset mechanism to turn the gas supply back on when the emergency is over. Models that have red shut-off buttons recessed into a metal frame minimize the possibility of an inadvertent shutoff. All emergency controls in the classroom should be readily accessible by the teacher, but not too easily reached by students.

Hot Water
Hot water is needed in science laboratories for safety reasons. Schools need to be mindful of the maximum temperature of the hot water and keep it well below the scalding point. Sanitizing splash-proof safety goggles, washing glassware, washing hands after working with chemicals or living specimens, and cleaning equipment for reuse all rely on the use of hot water. Some states require the use of soap and hot water in science laboratories as an effective and proven hygiene procedure that is environmentally friendly as well.

Eyewash and Safety Shower
An eyewash and a shower, both clearly marked, must be installed in every chemistry and physical science classroom, at a distance from every workstation of no more than 25 feet for the eyewash and 50 feet for the shower. They must have sufficient water pressure to

operate properly, and be kept free from obstructions at all times. The floor should have a drain and a trap so that the eyewash can be flushed regularly. The eyewash and shower should be separated sufficiently so that both can be used at the same time.

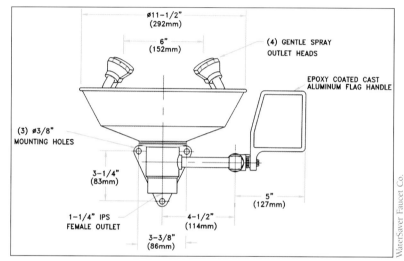

Figure 6. Wall-mounted dual eyewash.

One eyewash and shower in each room must meet ADA requirements, and they should also accommodate non-disabled persons. For example, there must be enough room for a non-disabled person to bend over to use the eyewash.

An eyewash that can wash both eyes simultaneously is required for any classroom, laboratory, and preparation room where hazardous chemicals are being used. Squeeze bottles and body drenches are not sufficient. The eyewash should provide an instant supply of fresh, aerated water with tempered flow for at least 15 minutes. A model that can stay

in the open position, leaving the user's hands free, is preferable.

The shower should be large enough to accommodate both an injured person and the person who is helping to wash the chemicals off the injured person. It should have a fixed valve handle or a chain with a large ring.

For more information on eyewashes and showers, see the American National Standards Institute (ANSI) standards for eyewash and shower equipment (Z358.1-1990).

Storage Facilities for Students
Individual storage facilities for students can be safety hazards. Separate, locking drawers for students, once the norm, have proven to be more of a problem than a benefit. Students can store dangerous materials in them, and separate locked storage spaces take a great deal of time to search in an emergency. Larger storage areas with separate bins are preferable.

Storage of Hazardous Chemicals
Secure storage of chemicals is a major safety and legal consideration in science facilities design. Chemical storage rooms should have lockable, fireproof doors that open outward. Chemicals should never be stored in class-

rooms or areas that students frequent or to which they have access. Hazardous chemicals should not be stored in the preparation room, nor in the equipment storage room or where sensitive equipment or electrical shutoffs are located.

Provision should be made in the preparation room for a spark-free laboratory refrigerator.

Drop ceilings should not be used in rooms where chemicals are stored because they may allow easy breaches of security in these potentially dangerous areas. Many accidents in which students are seriously hurt occur after they have stolen chemicals that were stored in insecure areas. Tort law tends to hold schools liable for not providing better security for chemicals, because it is negligent to fail to provide secure and safe storage for chemicals. Planning this type of storage is relatively easy to do during the early phases of the design process.

Space for safe storage of chemicals should be at least 1 square foot per student, which counts as part of the 10 square foot minimum per student recommended for preparation and storage. For example, a laboratory designed for 24 students should have approximately 240 square feet of preparation and storage area, including at least 24 square feet for a separate chemical storage room. More chemical storage space may be needed in schools where advanced chemistry is taught.

The chemical storage room or closet must have enough space to allow the storage of chemicals in compatible groups and with sufficient distance between incompatible chemicals. For example, nitric acid must be stored separately from organics.

Commercial companies have developed storage systems designed for proper chemical storage. Secure, specialized storage units for acids, flammables, and corrosives are available. An approved, grounded, and dedicated flammables cabinet or safety can must be provided. Any chemicals not kept in a separate chemical storage area should be kept in a dedicated, lockable cabinet. Storing chemicals alphabetically instead of by compatibility is extremely hazardous.

Shelves and cabinets for chemical storage must be attached to the wall for stability. Wooden shelves, plastic shelf supports, or other materials that resist corrosion will prevent the collapse of shelves loaded with chemicals. The supports must be spaced closely enough to prevent the shelves from sagging. The shelves should be at most 12 inches deep, so that the chemicals cannot be stored more than two containers deep. Space chemical containers so that each one can be reached easily without knocking over adjacent containers. Lips on the edges of shelves help prevent the containers from falling.

The chemical storage area is to be used for storage only and not as an occupied space.

It is vital to place chemical inventories and material safety data sheets (MSDSs), which list the properties and hazards of the chemicals, in accessible locations outside chemical storage rooms as well as inside them. The school nurse and administrator will also need copies. These records inform fire and safety personnel concerning what is being stored, so that they can assess the potential for combustion ahead of time. Most jurisdictions require that MSDSs be readily accessible to users.

Ventilation

The ventilation system is another major design consideration, particularly for a renovation. Generally, older school buildings were not air-conditioned and often relied on gravity ventilation and open windows for cooling. Public buildings are not heated and cooled as closed systems. Their constant intake of approximately 15 percent outside air contributes to a healthy environment, though it adds to heating costs. An architect or HVAC engineer will calculate the percentage of outside air that needs to be brought in continuously and how long it takes to circulate all of the air in the classroom.

Forced ventilation at a minimum rate of four changes of air per hour should be provided for science laboratories, and continuous ventilation at six changes per hour for chemical storage rooms. Assuming that there is a fume hood in each preparation room, four air changes per hour is adequate. A room used to house animals may require continuous ventilation at four changes per hour. All exhausts should be vented to the outside of the building, not recirculated in the building's ventilation system.

Chemical storage rooms need systems that vent directly outside, usually to the roof, and away from fresh-air intake pipes. Storage cabinets for flammables should not be ventilated; however, corrosives cabinets should be ventilated to the outside.

Every science room should be equipped with exhaust fans designed for the rapid venting of smoke or bad odors created by an investigation. These small units often replace a windowpane and are controlled by an on/off switch on a nearby wall. They should be equipped with fan guards.

For more information on ventilation, see the ANSI standards for laboratory ventilation (Z9.5-1992) and consult the American Society of Heating, Refrigerating, and Air-Conditioning Engineers (ASHRAE) standards.

Fume Hoods

A fume hood is required for every chemistry, physical science, or other science laboratory where hazardous or vaporous chemicals are used. Advanced chemistry classes generally need two, and these must be separated by several feet. Fume hoods are not needed at the elementary level and only rarely at the middle school level. However, most middle schools need a fume hood in the preparation room.

Fume hoods require make-up air systems to replace the room air that they remove. The systems can be an integral part of the building's ventilation system or part of the installed hood. In the latter case, they should operate automatically when the hood fan is turned on and provide the appropriate amount of exhaust at the right time.

The hood must exhaust directly to the outdoors, preferably through a stainless-steel duct that runs to the roof of the building and vents at a sufficient distance from any air intake to prevent the recirculation of exhaust air. The correct separation distance depends on the physical configuration of the building and should be calculated by an HVAC engineer.

The hood should provide a minimum of

Free-standing fume hood in a high school laboratory. (10)

80 linear feet of airflow per minute at its face with the sash open 6 inches above the bench or counter. The sash level should be marked for 100 linear feet of airflow per minute, with the date of the last measurement.

A free-standing hood with four transparent sides, only one of which is operable, may be used to enable students to work in small groups or gather around an experiment.

Some schools install individual down-draft fume hoods at each student workstation, but these have poor ventilation and fume-removal capabilities, and the loss of working space is a disadvantage. Ductless hoods are never recommended.

At least one hood should be designed to comply with the ADA accessibility guidelines.

For more information on fume hoods, see sections 5.6.1 and 5.6.2 of the ANSI standards for laboratory ventilation (Z9.5-1992). Consult the ASHRAE (ANSI/ASHRAE) 110-1985 standards and be sure that all hoods meet the 4.0 AU 0.10 standard for testing fume hoods.

Fire Protection

When science facilities are built, walls between the classrooms and hallways are usually extended above the ceiling, providing effective fire protection for the hallways for as long as an hour. Fire-rated corridor doors are generally required. Dead-end hallways should be no more than 20 feet long. Fire alarm systems that use light signals to aid hearing impaired students are usually mandatory. Local and state fire codes should be met or exceeded.

Local government building and fire officials can provide information on the need for sprinklers, smoke detectors, and specific types of

Safety shower, eyewash, and fume hood. (11)

fire extinguishers, and have discretion when codes don't specify requirements for science rooms and laboratories.

Sprinkler systems are usually required in buildings with over 20,000 square feet of floor space and are recommended for laboratories and for preparation and storage rooms. Fire protection in science storage rooms is usually achieved by maintaining careful practices and installing sprinklers, as well as smoke and heat detectors and monitoring systems. If sprinklers are present, separate, protected storage must be planned for water-reactive chemicals. See NFPA Standard 45 (1996) guidelines.

Other Factors

Additional factors that contribute to safety include adequate lighting, suitable areas for dispensing chemicals safely, and the provision of safety guards and equipment. Laboratory layout should be conducive to the supervision of students, and windows in offices, preparation rooms, and student project rooms will facilitate visual supervision of the students. Good communication systems, such as telephones or two-way public address systems, and emergency call systems, are essential for maintaining a safe environment.

Special Precautions for Seismic Areas

Designing or renovating a facility in an area subject to earthquakes, poses additional problems. A recent earthquake in Northridge, California, demonstrated that vertical ground motion can have a devastating effect. Items on shelves bounced up and down and fell off, which means that lips or guardrails on shelves, which are mandatory in seismically active areas and normally increase safety, did not succeed in keeping the items in place. Beakers and storage canisters should be stored in recessed cabinet frames so that they will be held in during vertical motion. This motion may also cause the sliding doors on cabinets to fall out of their tracks unless the top and bottom guides are deep enough to prevent it.

In areas of seismic activity, it is particularly important that heavy items not be stored on open shelving or on top of wall cabinets. Expensive equipment such as computers and countertop apparatus should be clamped or bolted down, and tall storage cabinets should be bolted to the walls to prevent their overturning. Light fixtures and other items that hang from the ceiling must be suspended separately and braced diagonally above the ceiling.

Particular attention needs to be paid to the strength of the walls and the weight-bearing capacity of the floors when rolling shelves are used in seismically active areas. In an earthquake, these shelf units can generate enough momentum to roll quickly in one direction, crashing into the stationary end unit. If the walls are built of metal studs and drywall, or of unreinforced masonry, the rolling units can crash through them. The shelves should be kept clamped to their rails at all times, except when they are in use.

Connections for gas lines in seismically active areas should be flexible.

Problems Specific to Renovations

When science laboratory storage for chemicals, equipment and materials is being designed or renovated, the three most important elements to consider are safety, protection from fire, and easy evacuation from the classroom.

These objectives may be difficult to accomplish. Older buildings, most built without sufficient exits, fire barriers, and storage areas, will be subject to the latest building and fire codes as soon as structural alterations are

started. The designer should keep in close touch with government building officials, fire marshals, and state fire inspectors to ensure that the proposed alterations and additions conform to code and to best practice in fire safety.

Renovating older buildings may bring to light hazards not anticipated when construction plans were made. For example, asbestos may have been installed in an old building before it was considered to be a hazardous material, and it may not yet have been removed through an abatement process. Asbestos removal is extremely expensive. Raising a carpet or a layer of tile only to find asbestos tiles, or opening a wall and discovering asbestos-wrapped pipes, always results in increased construction costs. Time is also a concern, as the abatement process must be supervised by trained consultants and cannot be carried out while students are in school.

ADA Guidelines

Since good science experiences are important for students, they must be available to all students. Restricting disabled or physically challenged students to different facilities is illegal. The obligation to accommodate persons with disabilities increases when renovations are planned.

The 1997 Individuals with Disabilities in Education Act (IDEA) defines the rights of special education students in U.S. schools. IDEA mandates the inclusion of students with disabilities in school programming more clearly than ever before. All science classrooms should be built to accommodate every student who chooses to study in them. Providing wheelchair access, communication devices for hearing-impaired students, and Braille assistance for blind students in regular science classrooms are factors that must be considered when we build today's facilities. Co-teaching by special educators in the regular classroom is becoming more common and is being incorporated into best practice, since it is difficult to prove that studying a laboratory science in a special education classroom provides equal opportunity to learn.

The Americans with Disabilities Act of 1990 (ADA) defines standards for physical access to facilities for all persons, including students and teachers who use public buildings. For purposes of the act, a handicap is defined as a "determinable physical or mental characteristic of an individual which may result from disease, injury, congenital condition of birth, or functional disorder which is unrelated to the individual's qualifications for employment or promotion."

Guidelines for applying the ADA are found in the *Americans with Disabilities Act Accessibility Guidelines for Buildings and Facilities* (ADAAG). They are enforced by the Department of Justice. Because the ADAAG regulations are not specific to science facilities, some interpretation is required. The recommendations in this book include regulations and adaptations of related guidelines.

Generally, architects are familiar with the basic requirements of accessibility. Many schools built before 1990 are not accessible to disabled persons. While these schools may remain compliant by making reasonable progress toward expanded access, they have

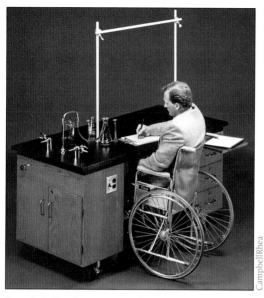

A workstation for students with physical disabilities. (12)

an obligation to provide complete accessibility when they start a renovation. Typical deficiencies found in older buildings include steps, narrow doors and aisles, a lack of elevators, workstations that cannot be used by a student in a wheelchair, and controls that require movements that are not possible for people with disabilities.

The ADA requires that existing deficiencies be corrected as each area in the building is renovated. A percentage of the renovation costs must be spent on upgrading the rest of the building along the path of travel from the entrance to the renovated space. Doors and aisles must be wide enough for wheelchairs—32 inches for doorways and 36 inches for aisles— toilet facilities must be wheelchair-accessible, and emergency facilities must be built at ap-

propriate heights in all new construction.

Every area of the school used by any student must have access for physically disabled persons built in during new construction. A person in a wheelchair should be able to move without assistance from the parking lot to every essential area of the school.

In science laboratories, this often means adjusting the height of some laboratory facilities and sinks, widening aisles, and relocating equipment.

The dimensions given in the following are the adult requirements, which apply to high schools.

Laboratory workstations. Many equipment manufacturers have developed workstations with lowered decks and lever, push-button, or electronic controls that can be used in place of regular laboratory stations to accommodate disabled students. These stations may be equipped with water, gas, electrical power, and sockets for apparatus rods. Controls should not require tight grasping, pinching, twisting of the wrist, or exerting more than 5 pounds of force to operate. If mobile workstations and portable equipment

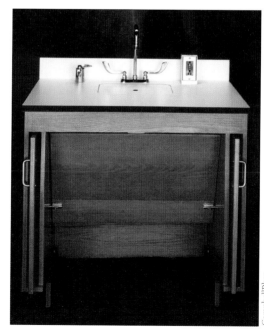

A sink for the physically disabled. (13)

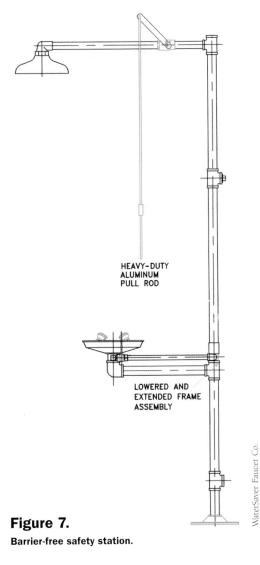

Figure 7.
Barrier-free safety station.

WaterSaver Faucet Co.

are used, space to accommodate them should be provided in every laboratory.

Laboratory sinks. Laboratory sinks are a special challenge, because the ADAAG specifies a sink depth of no more than 6 1/2 inches, so that a wheelchair can fit under the sink without having the sink be too high; the sink's rim must be at a maximum height of 34 inches for adult students. This leaves little space for a heavy sink assembly. A minimum vertical knee space of 27 inches and knee-space width of 30 inches are prescribed. The sinks must have lever-controlled faucets or a similar alternative.

Fume hoods. Fume hood manufacturers have lagged behind; they have lowered decks to the necessary 34-inch maximum, but many have not yet developed the necessary controls. Knee space requirements for seating at a fume hood are the same as for sinks.

Safety showers and eyewashes. The standard emergency shower/eyewash unit has the eyewash bowl mounted 38 inches above the floor, and the pull handle for the shower at about 68 inches above the floor. Assuming that the shower can be side-accessed, these can be modified to approximately 32 to 34 inches and 54 inches, respectively, to accommodate disabled students as well as the other students. The objective is to have the eyewash spout height at a maximum of 36 inches above the floor, the standard for a drinking fountain. If there is a second shower or eyewash in the room, these may be at standard heights.

Other adaptations. Wall cabinet locations are a potential hazard for students and teachers with disabilities, particularly to those who are visually impaired. Sharp or unexpected corners should be avoided, and all upper cabinets should have base cabinets beneath them. It is always advisable to build in wiring for communication equipment for hearing impaired students, so that electronic aids can be installed easily.

Some guidelines for children 12 years old or younger are also available, but they are not yet enforceable:

- *Eyewashes.* The spout height maximum is 30 inches above the floor, as for the water fountain standard. The eyewash bowl might be mounted 24 to 26 inches above the floor.
- *Sinks.* The maximum height of the sink rim is 31 inches. Apron and knee clearance are 24 inches, minimum.
- *Tables and counters.* Table and counter height should be 26 to 30 inches above the floor.

Creating a barrier-free learning environment benefits every learner in the school community. For planning teams, the key factor to remember is that accessibility for students with disabilities is mandatory.

Information Sources

Title II of the ADA requires public schools to comply with either the ADAAG or the Uniform Federal Accessibility Guidelines (UFAS). Independent schools must follow ADAAG requirements.

For help in applying ADAAG regulations to specific design issues, contact the Justice Department's technical assistance hot line at 1-800-514-0301. The web site is http://www.usdoj.gov/crt/ada/adahom1.htm. Also consult the state ADA accessibility office to determine state requirements.

Information is also available from the Office of Technical and Information Services, Architectural and Transportation Barriers Compliance Board (also known as the Access Board), 1331 F Street, NW, Suite 1000, Washington, DC 20004-1111, Telephone: 1-800-872-2253 or 202-272-5434. Documents can be accessed at www.access-board.gov/.

Publications are available, including

- a publications checklist (Document G-08)
- the *Uniform Federal Accessibility Standards* (UFAS) (Document S-04)
- Title III of the ADA, with the latest requirements from the Justice Department on the ADAAG (28 CFR 36, Appendix A; Document S-14)
- an updated reprint of the *Americans with Disabilities Act Accessibility Guidelines for Buildings and Facilities* (ADAAG), with new guidelines for building elements designed

for children's use (36 CFR 1191, Appendix A; Document S-08; Document S-30 for children's guidelines only). These new guidelines are not enforceable, because they have not yet been adopted by the Justice Department.

Minimizing Litigation

A key word in litigation is "reasonable": To avoid litigation, a reasonable effort to provide an environment that is safe for teachers and students is required. It is not necessary to design for protection from a worst-case scenario. For example, we wouldn't eliminate electrical outlets because a student could stick a piece of metal in one, but we do restrict their placement to appropriate locations and provide the necessary circuit breakers. It is our responsibility to ensure that space is adequate to promote safety, that class size is in the desired range, and that the architectural design enables teachers to exercise close supervision.

The question therefore is, How do we limit risks without undermining science learning? Fortunately, an abundance of information is available on this subject from research, and some guidance from the record of tort law cases.

The Research Base

Planning teams and designers need to be well informed about the research base regarding accidents. Newspapers often publish reports on accidents in classrooms, since the accident rate in schools is 10 to 50 times higher than that of the chemical industry. Research goes beyond the headlines to look at the factors

that accompany school accidents, which include

- inadequate or poorly designed working space, overcrowding, and too few workstations
- teachers with poor course work preparation
- teachers who are teaching more than two preparations at the same time
- poor school discipline
- inadequate safety training

It is important to remember that many research studies were conducted before the greatly expanded use of technology in the classroom and the passage of the Individuals with Disabilities in Education Act of 1997. The significant impact of these two factors on the amount of space required for a safe and effective science learning environment should be taken into consideration when planning facilities.

Tort Law

A tort is a wrong or injury to a person or property not involving a breach of contract. The standard of proof is a preponderance of evidence. The burden of proof rests with the plaintiff, who must establish that the preponderance of evidence shows that the defendant occasioned the damage. A reasonable person is expected to foresee possible injury arising out of the foibles of human nature and to be able to anticipate difficulties.

Negligence is defined as conduct that falls below a standard of care established by law to protect others against unreasonable risk of harm. Educators are expected to minimize risk of harm. The law requires only that reason-

able and common sense decisions be made to promote safe working and learning conditions for the staff and students. There are levels of risk in the school environment, as in all areas of everyday living, that have to be tolerated, yet that permit reasonably safe, positive, and optimum learning. The goal is to promote maximum safety in order to prevent injury to people and damage to property.

A finding of negligence usually involves one of the following:

- misconduct, committing an unlawful act, or doing what should not have been done—in this case, the performance of an act that places students in danger
- the failure to do what should be done—here, failing to take the necessary action to protect students

Providing inadequate facilities, allowing a lack of proper facilities, and mandating curricula when facilities are inadequate for them can result in a finding of negligence, as in *Bush v. Oscoda.* (See box.)

The following are additional examples of litigation involving school facilities.

Maxwell v. Santa Fe Public Schools, 1975. A school board, but not the teacher, was held liable for a student injury because eye protection was not available.

Reagh v. San Francisco Unified School District, 1953. A school district was held liable for in-

> **Bush v. Oscoda Area Schools, 1981**
>
> A 14-year-old girl was burned severely when a plastic jug of alcohol that she was carrying exploded. The jug was used to transport alcohol to fill portable burners in a science class being taught in a non-science classroom. The school was found liable for the injuries, because the class was held in a non-science classroom and no safety devices were available, which meant that the facility had not been properly designed or equipped for science teaching. The court found against the teacher for reasons of inappropriate supervision and against the principal for scheduling an experimental curriculum in a classroom with inadequate facilities. The court awarded damages from the teacher and the principal.

juries that resulted from chemicals' being kept on an open shelf rather than in a secure area.

In some states, public employees may be held liable only for gross negligence, and the burden of proof is on the litigant.

Allowing poorly designed facilities that do not provide a safe working environment due to any of the following causes may result in litigation:
- inadequate space
- poor ventilation
- conditions that lead to poor supervision of students
- lack of safety eyewashes, safety showers, or alarm systems
- lack of adequate lighting or chemical storage
- unsafe electrical outlets

Asking teachers to work in unventilated spaces, violating the Occupational Safety and Health Act (OSHA), and forcing a student to take an unnecessary risk, such as moving chemicals from room to room because of inadequate storage facilities, are some of the acts that might result in a finding of negligence.

The newspaper story "Teacher Falling into Acid" (1989), shows how a failure to provide a safety shower led to a serious injury that might easily have resulted in litigation.

Best Practice
No facility can be completely accident-proof. The way to minimize risk is to follow the precepts of best practice. School districts and planning teams should consider recommendations found in professional publications concerning designing facilities that provide the safest working and learning environments for teachers and students. The expectation is that planners will have a reasonable awareness of student behavior and anticipate the difficulties that might arise, so that they can design facilities that do not present unsafe environments. Besides reviewing the research base, consulting with experienced school architects, suppliers, and other consultants should prove helpful. Above all, the principles behind creating safe and effective instructional spaces should be given priority in the budget and the planning process.

"Teacher Falling into Acid"

A science teacher, working alone after school to prepare chemicals for the next day's instruction, dropped a bottle of concentrated sulfuric acid, slipped on the spilled acid, and fell backward onto a large piece of broken glass and into the puddle of acid. She called for help, and a colleague carried her to a gymnasium shower because there was no safety shower in the entire science area. She suffered severe burns, made worse by the delay in rinsing off the acid.

References

Americans with Disabilities Act Accessibility Guidelines for Buildings and Facilities. (1991, July 26). *Federal Register,* 56(144).

Architectural and Transportation Barriers Compliance Board. (1992). *Americans with Disabilities Act Accessibility Guidelines for Buildings and Facilities.* Washington, DC: Author.

Bush v. Oscoda Area Schools, 109 Mich.App. 373, 311 N.W.2d 788 (Mich.App. 1981)

Emergency Eyewash and Shower Equipment (ANSI Standard Z358.1-1990). (1990). New York: American National Standards Institute.

Fire Protection for Laboratories Using Chemicals (NFPA Standard 45). (1996). Quincy, MA: National Fire Protection Association.

Laboratory Ventilation (ANSI Standard Z9.5-1992). (1992). New York: American National Standards Institute.

Life Safety Code (NFPA Standard 101). (1977). Quincy, MA: National Fire Protection Association.

Maxwell v. Santa Fe Public Schools, 87 N.M. 383, 534 P.2d 307 (1975)

Method of Testing Performance of Laboratory Fume Hoods (ANSI/ASHRAE Standard 110-1985). (1985). Atlanta, GA: American Society of Heating, Refrigerating, and Air-Conditioning Engineers.

National Science Teachers Association. (1998). Laboratory Science (1990 position statement). In *NSTA Handbook 1998–99* (pp. 194–197). Arlington, VA: Author.

Reagh v. San Francisco Unified School District, 119 Cal.App.2d 65, 259 P.2d 43 (1953)

Teacher Falling into Acid. (1989, March 3). *Lubbock Avalanche Journal,* p. 4C.

Young, John R. (1972). A Second Survey of Safety in Illinois High School Laboratories. *Journal of ChemEd,* 49(1), 55.

For additional resources, see the bibliography.

CHAPTER 4

Designing Facilities for the Elementary School (K–5)

Elementary school programs vary widely. Some schools prefer using teams of teachers, whose members can specialize, while others stress the integration of subjects by offering all content instruction in the self-contained classroom. Whichever of these approaches is taken will influence decisions concerning the settings for instruction. But because trends will always change, even within the same school system, the challenge to those charged with creating elementary facilities is to plan for the present with an eye toward the future.

The most basic decision at the elementary level is whether to build separate science facilities or to make all classrooms—or one of each shared pair of classrooms—science-friendly.

Most schools that have the resources opt to do both, putting the basics for science in every room, while creating a special space for more in-depth discovery. This approach facilitates science's integration with other subjects, while stressing the unique characteristics of the science environment.

Whether science is taught in the general classroom or in a dedicated science room, the facility demands are similar, with space, flexibility, and safety among the most important considerations. The following sections offer detailed suggestions and information for designing and equipping these learning environ-ments and for providing the other resources that a good science program requires.

Space Requirements, Room Design

To accommodate current technology needs and teaching practices,

- a good science room will require a minimum of 40 square feet of floor space per student, or 960 square feet for 24 students
- a multiple-use classroom in which science is taught will require a minimum of 45 square feet of floor space per student, or 1,080 square feet for 24 students
- an additional 10 square feet of space per student will be needed for preparation space for the teacher and separate storage space (240 square feet for a class of 24)

The 1990 NSTA Position Statement on laboratory science recommends a maximum class size of 24 students in elementary school.

An additional 15 square feet is needed for each computer station and approximately 20 square feet to accommodate a student with disabilities.

For safety and flexibility, a rectangular room at least 30 feet wide, without alcoves, is rec-ommended. A ceiling height of 10 feet is de-sirable. The science room should have two

A terrarium in an elementary science classroom. (14)

locking entrances, doorways that accommo-date students with physical disabilities, and adequate ventilation.

The Multiple-Use Classroom

In the early years—pre-kindergarten through grades 2 or 3—science should be integrated with other subjects and activities throughout the day. The self-contained classroom will require plenty of table and floor surfaces where messy activities can be conducted easily. Sinks and counters at student-height are also needed, so that frequent hand-washing and clean-up can be accomplished with minimal assistance.

In the upper elementary grades (3 through 5), the classroom should have a greater capacity to accommodate science activities, even if some of those activities will be performed in a dedicated science room. Provision should be made to integrate science into classroom projects by providing sinks, flat surfaces, electricity, data jacks, video hookups, and provisions for overnight storage of projects in the classroom.

Furnishings

All multiple-use classrooms used for science will need:
- movable, flat-topped tables of appropriate size for the students
- a large sink with hot and cold water, mounted at student height, with space for a hand-held eyewash
- additional sinks or "wet areas"
- counters, base and wall cabinets, and shelves to house science-related equipment and materials
- some form of lockable storage
- tote-tray storage units or carts
- a chalkboard or marker board and tackable wall surfaces for displaying charts and posters, photographs, and maps.

- a projection screen and LCD projector
- electrical outlets with ground-fault-interrupter (GFI) protection
- network connections for computers, including at least one adjacent to the science cabinets

Many of the suggestions and ideas presented below for room arrangements and furnishings for specialized science classrooms apply to multiple-use classrooms as well.

The Specialized Science Classroom

As enthusiasm for science grows, so do the expectations of students and teachers. Some schools are lucky enough to have a science specialist, but even if such a staff member is not available, the existence of a special space for extended exploration is always desirable. The elementary science laboratory, often called the "discovery room," is a large, well-equipped, and well-lit classroom with sinks and extensive storage for science equipment and kits. These materials may be used in the room or checked out for follow-up activities in the homeroom. While a discovery-room approach requires cooperation and schedule coordination among the elementary staff, most teachers feel that the advantages of this specialized science room outweigh any administrative requirements.

Because of differences in both the students and their science programs, there are advantages to having separate science classrooms for kindergarten through second-grade students and for third- through fifth-grade students, although the facilities are very similar. The furnishings for each are described below.

Furnishings (K–2)

The type and arrangement of space desirable for students in kindergarten through second grade requires great flexibility. Fixed student workstations should be avoided in favor of flat-topped, movable tables. For safety reasons, there should always be a minimum of 4 feet between the perimeter counters and the tables. It is important for planners to verify that the floor space will be suitable for small-group arrangements around a central, movable teacher's table, as well as for traditional classroom seating and other seating arrangements. Allow at least 4 feet on all sides around each grouping of tables. In the classroom-type arrangement, provide a minimum of 8 feet from the front wall of the classroom to the first row of tables. The teacher will then be able to move around easily, have the use of a table, instruct at the board, and use a projector.

Sinks (K–2)

Several sinks with tall, swivel faucets should be inset in the student-height, perimeter countertops. The number of sinks depends on the number of students and the types of activities that are expected to require sinks. A good rule of thumb for kindergarten through second grade is one sink for every four to six stu-

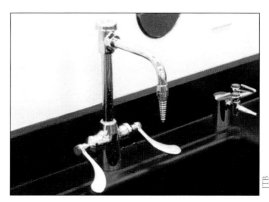

Swivel faucet. (15)

dents. Standard stainless-steel kitchen sinks are acceptable, but they should be large—16 by 20 inches, for example—and have fairly deep bowls. It is best to provide hot and cold water at all sinks, for safe hygiene. A drinking fountain and dual eyewash can be provided at one sink and a hand-held, pullout drench shower at another.

The teacher will need a portion of counter

Hand-held, pullout eyewash. (16)

space at least 6 feet long and an adjacent large sink at the standard adult standing height of 36 inches.

Work Space (K–2)

The height of counters along the classroom perimeter should be 24 inches. It may be necessary to provide some variety of counter height to accommodate students of different heights.

In order to allow the flat-topped tables to be level when they are pushed together and

Flat-topped tables that can be arranged in different configurations. (17)

to compensate for variations in students' size, adjust the tables to the same height and order chairs or stools of various heights. A good height for the tables is 20 inches. Square tables, 30 inches on a side, work well, as do rectangular ones that are small enough to be moved easily, yet large enough to permit students to spread out their work. Chairs or stools

can be used for seating. Many teachers prefer stools without backs, because they can be pushed under the tables when not in use, freeing up floor space.

The teacher should have a movable table in which materials may be stored. At this level, the table rarely needs utilities.

Storage (K–2)

Casework should include base cabinets with student-level counters along two walls for additional work and preparation space. Wall cabinets should be placed above all base cabinets for safety reasons. Most counters will be 24 inches deep, the others, generally 30 inches. Even if chemicals and cleaning supplies are to be stored in another room, teachers will want some lockable classroom cabinets, because even relatively innocuous materials such as glues and paints can tempt students and result in poisoning.

All countertops in classrooms, preparation rooms, and storerooms should have plastic laminate or other durable finishes resistant to water and mild chemicals. Countertops near a water source should have a splash back with no seams. Give priority to selecting high-quality cabinets made of marine-grade plywood with plastic laminate fronts. Avoid particleboard assembly, because this material reacts poorly to moisture. Flexible storage can be provided by a variety of cabinets with drawers and doors of different sizes. Leaving a 30- to 36-inch-wide space under a counter will allow students a place to sit at the counter.

Low-level casework. (18)

K–5

Compartmental storage cabinet. (19)

One or two tall science storage cabinets, separate from the teacher's personal cabinet and bolted to the wall, will store items of various sizes, especially if it has vertical dividers that hold adjustable shelves. This cabinet should lock. Hinged doors are recommended for wall cabinets, because sliding doors waste about 3 inches of cabinet depth. Typical depths for these cabinets are 12 and 15 inches.

Mounting heights for wall cabinets will depend on whether students are to have access to them: 42 inches from the floor for students, 54 inches for adults. All cabinets should have positive latches that can withstand seismic events without opening. Some cabinets also must meet the Americans with Disabilities Act Accessibility Guidelines (ADAAG). At least 18 linear feet of book shelving, 10 or more inches deep, some at student height and some at adult height, should be provided.

It is important to set aside a suitable area for hats and coats so they will not be in the way. Large storage bins with lids for recycling paper, cans, and bottles are also a good idea. Window shelves are desirable to accommodate plants, terrariums, aquariums, and small animal cages. Aquariums are often placed on perimeter countertops.

Shelving for equipment. (20)

Display Space (K–2)

One wall should be kept largely free of cabinets to allow places to display students' artwork and instructional aids like maps, charts, and posters. Tackboards can be hung in any unused wall space, and tack strips can be installed above cabinets.

Dry-erase marker boards are fast becoming standard, because chalk dust can be harmful to both computers and people. However, there is also a concern about the toxicity of the markers, and all manufacturers' information should be studied. Sliding, multiple-panel boards can be used to extend the marker board without increasing the amount of wall space used. Marker boards come in several colors, and even "permanent" inks can be erased using alcohol or nail polish remover, both of which are highly flammable. Water-based inks are preferable. If a marker board is to be used by students, it should be mounted with the bottom edge 24 inches above the floor. As this is an uncomfortable height for most adults, the board should be taller than standard height to accommodate adults.

The instructional focus area must support a variety of presentation formats, including video, laser disc, slides, projected microscope images, overhead projection, and dry experiments. Controls, including light switches, can be installed—often wall-mounted—in the

Multiple-panel marker board. (21)

front of the room, easily accessible to the teacher.

A projection screen should be mounted on a wall or the ceiling. The screen size should be at least 5 feet by 7 feet, but 6 feet by 8 feet is preferable. If the screen is to be mounted on a high ceiling, include an additional "tail" at the top of the screen; the bottom of the screen will then be approximately 4 feet above the floor.

Marker boards do not make good projection screens, because their surfaces do not reflect light well.

Utilities (K–2)

Electrical power should be installed with ground-fault interrupters (GFI) on every circuit.

Provide plenty of duplex electrical outlets and data outlets around the perimeter of the room for the movable tables that are brought close to them when power is needed. Overhead, pull-down electric cords similar to those used in automotive shops or power poles can supply power to the middle of the room, but must be used with extra caution. Power poles are inflexible and generally cannot stand much physical abuse.

Care should be taken to investigate the safety

Overhead pull-down cords similar to those used in automotive shops. (22)

Power poles, which are the least flexible alternative and are generally not resistant to physical abuse. (23)

features of any alternative to wall outlets and to ensure that everyone, including custodial staff, is informed of procedures for their safe use.

Allow one 20-amp circuit for every three computers to be used in the classroom.

Gas is not used at this level. Flattop hot plates and a microwave oven for the teacher's use are standard equipment. The microwave oven is best located in the preparation room, for safety reasons.

The emergency shut-off controls for water and electrical service should be near the teacher's station, not far from the door, and not easily accessible to students.

A room exhaust fan will be needed when an investigation or demonstration creates

Room exhaust fan. (24)

smoke or an unpleasant odor. Exhaust fans are often installed in place of a windowpane.

Lighting and Darkening Rooms (K–2)

A bright elementary classroom needs at least 50 foot-candles per square foot of floor surface and 75 to 100 foot-candles at the work surface. Lighting design must be handled carefully to avoid washing out projected images while providing enough light to enable students to see their tabletops. If computers are to be used in the room, directional diffusers are recommended, and the downlighting on the work surface can be provided by three-tube parabolic flourescent fixtures with switches that allow the room to be darkened in stages from front to back. Pendant, indirect fluorescent fixtures supplemented with compact, low-voltage downlights also work well in rooms with computers, but not as well with projectors.

Room darkening can be accomplished with blinds or shades. At this grade level, blinds are probably sufficient to darken the room for video projection. Some new schools are being constructed with bulletin boards that are rolled across the windows to darken the room.

Computers (K–2)

Today, students are learning to do research electronically from the earliest grades. Most new schools are being built with four to six data jacks for computer networking in every classroom, whether or not the school has adequate hardware on hand. Computers may be mounted permanently on low countertops, away from the faucets, or moved into the room

Recessed parabolic fluorescent lighting fixture. (25)

Pendant, indirect, three-tube fluorescent lighting fixture. (26)

Figure 8.

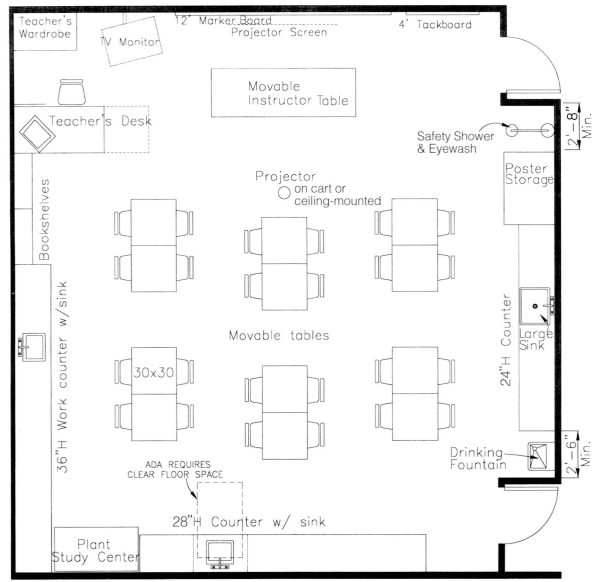

Primary multiple-use classroom, K–2.

on rolling carts as needed.

Laptop computers can be plugged into data jacks, then stored in cabinets and recharged when not in use, allowing safe, secure computer use in the classroom while reducing costs and saving space.

Furnishings (3–5)

Classroom needs are somewhat different for third- through fifth-grade students, not only because the students are taller than the younger students, but because their developmental needs are different and their curriculum is more demanding. In the upper elementary grades, it is even more important for science classes to be held daily.

The arrangement of the science room should be similar to that for the younger elementary students. However, at the fourth- and fifth-grade levels, students often attempt large and long-term projects and conduct independent investigations. Because these activities may involve building tall structures on the floor, ample floor space and storage space for use between classes should be provided.

For more information and details on the following, consult the earlier section on furnishings.

Sinks (3–5)

Perimeter countertops at student height should have one sink for every four or five students. Provide one sink and an adjacent 6- to 8-

Acid dilution trap. (27)

K–5

"Rinseaway" sink. (28)

foot section of counter space, 36 inches high, for the teacher's use. Every sink should have hot and cold water. At least one must have wrist-blade handles and be accessible to disabled students.

Standard stainless-steel, single- or double-bowl kitchen sinks, 15 inches by 15 inches, with fairly deep bowls, at least 8 inches deep, may be used. They should have tall, swiveling faucets, and one of them should have a dual eyewash. Another possibility is the "rinseaway" sink: a molded fiberglass sloping top with raised edges and curved corners that drains to an integral sink. These units are ideal for messy cleanups and may provide the best location for a hand-held body drench that can also be used as a sprayer to clean up the sink. A plaster trap to catch sand or gravel that may otherwise be washed down the drain is a good idea.

Work Space (3–5)

For upper elementary students, 21- to 23-inch table heights and 27-inch high countertop heights are appropriate. Varying the seating height will help accommodate all students. Since science laboratory casework manufacturers do not usually provide cabinets for 27-inch counters, because 29 inches is the standard, some custom casework may be necessary. Again, flat-topped tables that can be moved easily and rearranged into a number of configurations are recommended. A good size for two-student tables is 24 by 48 inches. If apparatus rods are to be used, sockets may be provided for them in the countertops or tables, because standard plastic laminate countertops are too thick (1 1/2 inches) to accommodate most "C-clamp" apparatus rods.

Chairs, or stools without backs will provide adequate seating.

Storage (3–5)

At this level, countertops are usually plastic laminate, but if the science curriculum is going to include dyes or caustic chemicals, the more expensive resin top may be worth the higher cost. Base cabinets should have several configurations of drawers and doors, and one or more adjustable shelves inside. A 30- to 36-inch-wide knee space should be provided below some lowered counters, for student workstations. Map drawer units are often useful, but the countertops above them will have to be deeper than normal, usually at least 30 inches. Provide tall storage cabinets, wall cabinets, and bookshelves similar to those used in the younger grades. The appropriate mounting height for wall cabinets in this space

is 45 inches from the floor for students and 54 inches for adults.

Display Space (3–5)

Ceiling hooks or a 1-inch diameter steel pipe suspended from suitable structures above the ceiling tiles will provide places to hang various

Library card catalog unit. (31)

items. Each hook should have at least a 10-pound capacity, and the pipe should hold at least 200 pounds.

Utilities, Lighting and Darkening Rooms (3–5)

In general, provide the same wiring, utilities, and lighting as for the room for kindergarten through second grade, including a room exhaust fan and GFI protection on every electrical circuit.

Computers (3–5)

The classroom will need plenty of electrical power and data jacks, because it is likely to have several permanently stationed computers at the perimeter, as well as docking places for the computer carts.

Teacher's Space

In addition to the demonstration table, a desk with some shelves

Rolling tote-tray storage unit. (30)

A teacher's desk space in a preparation room. (29)

and a file cabinet in a room corner, or a desk in the preparation room, can serve as a "home space" for the science teacher. This area should be off-limits to the students. Make telephone, electrical power, and network jacks for a computer available at the desk. Many classrooms with network computer outlets keep a fast, powerful printer at the teacher's desk for use by the entire class.

Preparation and Storage Areas

Teachers need space to prepare activities at the beginning of the day for the different classes that will visit the science room. For kindergarten through second grade classes, this area should contain base cabinets with counters at adult height, a sink, and space for several rolling carts used to move chemicals and equipment in and out of the classroom. A refrigerator and a microwave oven are desirable. If windows occupy much of the exterior wall of the science room, provide additional storage space in the preparation area. Tote-tray storage units and cabinets with adjustable shelves allow teachers to store the items related to a particular lesson in a single container that can be pulled out at the appropriate time. Old library card catalog units are useful for holding small items in labeled compartments.

For grades 3 though 5, a separate preparation room next to the science room is desirable. A view window between the preparation room and science room facilitates supervision of students. The room should have base and wall cabinets; one or two tall, compartmentalized storage cabinets; a desk with a telephone and electrical and network connections; and counter space with a large sink, a spark-free refrigerator with an icemaker, and a microwave oven. The storage space needs open shelves. In seismically active areas, installing lips on the shelves will help prevent breakage and accidents. Adequate ventilation and safety equipment are required. Storage rooms provide needed security and specialized storage for large, expensive, or sensitive equipment.

Because hazardous materials are usually not used at these grade levels, special storage cabinets are seldom needed. A secure cabinet in the preparation area, 3 feet by 3 feet for the lower grades and larger for the upper grades, will suffice. If flammables such as alcohol in 1-gallon or larger containers are used, an appropriate storage cabinet should be available. In some cases, depending on the chemicals the curriculum calls for, a separate, secure, ventilated, storage closet for chemical storage may be needed.

Preparation and storage space for kindergarten through grade 2 and grades 3 to 5 can be shared successfully if the location is appropriate and sufficient space is provided for concurrent use.

For further information:

ADA requirements .... Chapter 3

Safety, fume hoods .... Chapter 3 & Appendix B

Outdoor facilities .... Chapter 7

Finishing materials .... Chapter 8

Projectors, screens, and other equipment .... Appendix D

CHAPTER 5

Designing Facilities for the Middle School (6–8)

While most middle school curricula emphasize integrating subjects, they also provide specialists who teach science. This means that students in the middle grades must change classes several times a day. A high-quality middle school science program requires science classrooms with laboratory space, and school designers must consider the distance the students will have to travel to these classes.

In traditional construction, science facilities were clustered in one wing of the school, bringing plumbing, gas, ventilation, and specialized fire protection together and reducing construction costs. In middle schools today, the "team" or "house" curriculum model is gaining in popularity. In this model, the student body is divided into large groups that share the same teachers for all of their basic subjects, and each group has its own classroom for most of these subjects.

Building a school to accommodate teaming is usually much more expensive, because it requires that science rooms, storage rooms, and other science facilities be replicated in each cluster. Some of this expense can be avoided by making the science facilities part of the central core of the building, easily accessible from each wing of the school. A building so designed can function in either curricular model, because the wings can be used to house the different teams or the different disciplines. If the science rooms must be decentralized and distributed among the houses, clustering rooms that need running water, such as science, fine arts, industrial arts, and consumer science rooms, with custodial closets and the cafeteria will help reduce costs.

Grouping Facilities for Integration

Whether the goal is to have separate departments, to team teach, or to be able to accommodate either model, planners will want to consider opportunities for integrating other subjects with science by grouping several facilities for science with related subjects such as math and applied sciences.

For example, many schools now include

A typical technology laboratory. (32)

computer-based technology laboratories that focus on careers in applied science. These laboratories can also be used to link many abstract science concepts to the real world. Because their electrical bus and ventilation requirements are similar to those of good science laboratories, technology rooms are particularly desirable neighbors for science rooms.

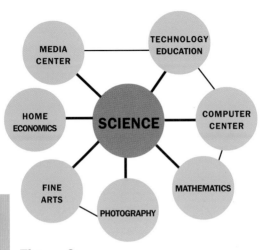

Figure 9.
Opportunities for integration.

Mathematics is the field most commonly integrated with science. When mathematics classrooms are located near the science area, interrelated projects that combine the two subjects can be developed and carried out in the science department's student project area. Mathematics programs especially benefit, because of their increased emphasis on hands-on activities in recent years.

Media production facilities also provide excellent opportunities for integration with the sciences. Student teams can develop and produce media programs, using equipment and resources from the science area and technology from the media center. With imagination, almost any room in the school can be designed as a potential location from which to broadcast to the rest of the school.

Finally, if consumer science, formerly known as home economics, is located close

to a science room, joint projects and investigations in the life sciences can be carried out in either space.

Space Requirements

Class size is an important design factor, because it helps determine the amount of space and number of workstations that will be needed. To accommodate current technology needs and teaching practices, a good science room will generally require

- a minimum of 45 square feet per student for a stand-alone laboratory, or 1,080 square feet for a class of 24 students
- a minimum of 60 square feet per student for a combination laboratory/classroom, or 1,440 square feet for a class of 24 students

The 1990 NSTA position statement on laboratory science recommends a maximum class size of 24 students in middle school.

An additional space of 15 square feet is required for each computer station, and another 20 square feet to accommodate each lab station for a student with disabilities. At least 10 square feet per student is needed for teacher preparation space and storage space.

Students using computers in the science laboratory. (34)

Space is also needed for longer-term student projects.

A ceiling height of 10 feet is desirable for a science room. The room should have at least two exits and doorways that accommodate students with physical disabilities.

There are several reasons why the middle school science classroom requires more space than the elementary science classroom. To begin with, student workstations in middle school are larger. Because activities are more prolonged and projects may extend over many class periods, space is needed where group and individual projects can be left in place for several days or weeks. Computer use is also greater at this level, so a greater allowance must be made for space for this activity.

Depending on the size of the school, at least one science room per grade level and one for every 120 students will be needed.

Middle school students conducting a science investigation. (33)

The Combination Laboratory/Classroom

Science rooms at the middle school level may be generic, allowing an integrated science program to be taught in any room, or they may be specialized. The trend is toward designing for flexibility, which allows changes in space allocation that often accompany enrollment growth, as well as future curriculum and technology needs.

Two models for middle-level science classrooms have proven particularly practical. Both are combination laboratory/classrooms. These are

1. A flexible room arrangement in which furniture is moved to accommodate either laboratory or direct instruction. Sinks and utilities are located along the perimeter of the room. This room arrangement allows a variety of configurations for laboratory and classroom work.

2. A room with fixed laboratory stations and a designated classroom area. This arrangement requires more floor space than a flexible room, because it has separate zones for each type of activity.

The greatest advantage of these two arrangements is that they provide ongoing access to laboratory activities for each class.

An important design consideration in either case is the room's ability to accommodate each type of instruction well. During direct instruction in the classroom model, all students need to face the instructor or the board. During laboratory activities, the teacher must have easy supervision of the students at their workstations.

For any room layout, always allow unobstructed aisle space of at least 4 feet between a counter or table and the areas set aside for general seating. There should be 8 feet between the front wall of the classroom and the first tables. An overcrowded room is a serious safety hazard.

A Flexible Room Arrangement

In the flexible laboratory/classroom, sinks and utilities are located on perimeter counters, and students use movable laboratory tables for both general classroom and laboratory work. This design provides maximum flexibility and makes the most efficient use of space.

Two tables, each seating two students on a side, form each workstation when placed adjacent to a counter. The tables, which are flat-topped, can be grouped to form flat surfaces

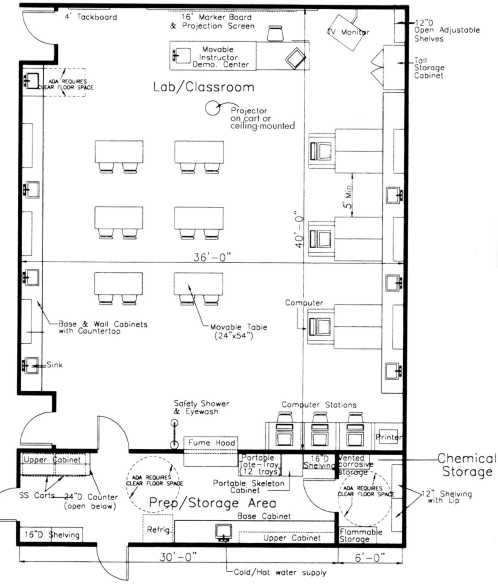

Figure 10. Flexible laboratory/classroom showing laboratory arrangement on right, classroom arrangement on left.

and rearranged to suit a variety of activities throughout the room.

Each group of four students has use of a sink, a source of heat, such as a hot plate, electric power for equipment and computers, and, often, network connections. The sinks should be installed in such as way that when tables are drawn up to the counters there will be enough

Flexible classroom:
a) Arranged for
classroom activities,
and
b) Arranged for
laboratory activities.
(35 and 36)

space between the tables for students to access the sinks easily.

A two-track, surface-mounted "raceway" may be installed above the counter's backsplash to bring in electric power and communications (data and television cable) outlets at regular intervals along the counter.

A Classroom Area and Fixed Workstations

A laboratory/classroom with freestanding utility islands makes it easy for the teacher to see all students during laboratory activities. The islands provide access to power and utilities and serve as workstations for four or more students. If the room is large, the islands may

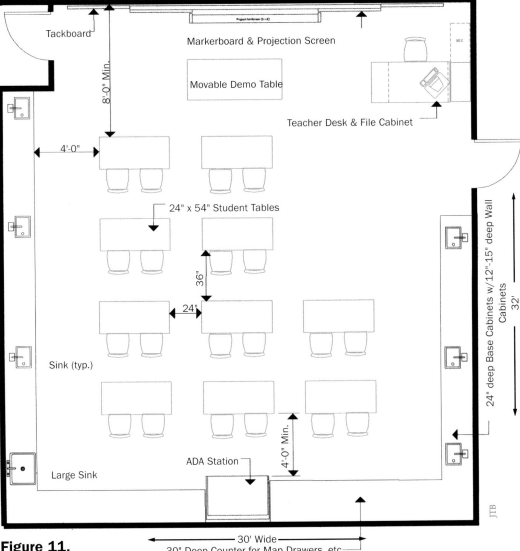

Tackboard

Markerboard & Projection Screen

Movable Demo Table

Teacher Desk & File Cabinet

8'-0" Min.

4'-0"

24" x 54" Student Tables

36"

24"

Sink (typ.)

24" deep Base Cabinets w/12"-15" deep Wall Cabinets

32'

4'-0" Min.

ADA Station

Large Sink

Figure 11.
30' Wide
30" Deep Counter for Map Drawers, etc.
Minimal middle school laboratory/classroom for 20 students.

be installed at one end of the room.

Trifacial (triple table hub) utility islands with large, deep sinks are frequently used.

These six-sided units do not include built-in work space. Instead, laboratory tables are drawn up to the three longer sides, creating work areas for groups of four students. The students share the central sink, which is accessed from the three narrower sides of the hub. Gas jets, electrical outlets, and computer data wiring are provided along the three longer sides. Each island can accommodate 12 students at either three large tables or six small ones. Two islands thus provide laboratory work space for 24 students.

The movable tables may also be combined and arranged in other configurations. Tables with electrical "pigtails" and outlets can be plugged into the trifacial unit, providing power

Students at a workstation. (37)

Patricia Strawbridge-PA

and data wiring at the far end of the table for computers and other electrical equipment.

A separate area provides movable seating for the classroom portion of the curriculum. Seating here can be at desk and chair combinations, tablet arm chairs, or the laboratory tables rearranged in a classroom format with stools or chairs.

The laboratory/classroom with fixed stations permits more in-depth laboratory experiences and promotes greater safety. However, this design is generally more expensive than the alternatives, because it requires significantly more space. In addition, the space becomes a permanent laboratory facility. Design teams will want to weigh the greater capacity for doing science against the loss of flexibility in the design.

Furnishings

The following describes the needs of a flexible laboratory/classroom with movable tables and perimeter counters, sinks, and utilities. With a few exceptions, the text also applies to laboratories and laboratory/classrooms with fixed stations.

Sinks

Sinks for student investigations should be fairly wide and deep and equipped with swiveling gooseneck faucets, that allow students to fill pails and large vessels under the faucet. The sink size should be at least 15 by 15 inches. A good rule of thumb is to provide one sink for four students. Resin sinks are preferable, because they resist chemical degradation. However, if corrosive chemicals are seldom used, stainless steel sinks with deep bowls may be acceptable as a money-saving measure. Hot water is desirable at all sinks and student workstations, for hygienic reasons.

Faucets should come equipped with aerators. Serrated nozzles adapted for the attachment of hoses are an option, but they cause an increase in water pressure and splatter water around the sink. If they cannot be unscrewed, teachers often respond by attaching a length of rubber hose to them to alleviate the problem.

It is also an advantage to have a large, deep sink with hot and cold water and adjacent counter space for various purposes, such as cleaning extra-large containers.

Two types of sinks that are very handy in middle school laboratories are

Faucet with serrated nozzle and hose. (38)

- a "rinseaway" sink, which has a 6- to 10-foot-long molded fiberglass tray with raised edges that slopes down to a sink basin, facilitating the clean up of plant and animal specimens and messy items. This tray accommodates experiments that need running water and a drain and require long-term storage. The sink may be equipped with a garbage disposal or a plaster trap to catch sand or gravel. A pullout eyewash sprayer on a hose can be used for cleaning up at the sink,

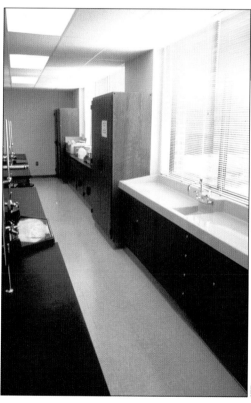

The "rinseaway" sink. (39)

The "slop" sink. (40)

Glassware drying rack. (41)

but cannot substitute for a dual eyewash.

- a deep, enameled-porcelain, wall-mounted janitor's slop sink, which is very useful for cleaning large containers and for filling deep vessels with water. Avoid the typical fixed faucet and opt for a swiveling, gooseneck one, because the fixed faucet reduces the open area of the bowl.

Glassware drying racks come in various sizes, and are often useful if installed above the perimeter sinks. Mount each rack so that it drains directly into the sink rather than down the wall. Request a high backsplash to protect the wall, so the drying rack can be mounted high enough above the sink to clear the faucet. Some teachers use a standard kitchen-counter drying rack, which can be removed and stored beneath the sink when not in use.

Work Space

For work space, counters 32 to 36 inches from the floor and tables 25 to 30 inches high are convenient for most students. It may be advantageous to vary the counter height somewhat, in order to accommodate all students.

Countertops should be made of epoxy resin or a similar chemical-resistant material. They should be caulked between the backsplash and the wall, and along any other joints, using clear silicone. Backsplashes 4 inches high are standard. Backsplashes should also run along the counter beside any tall cabinets and other surfaces that interrupt or are set into the counter space.

Movable laboratory tables should be approximately 54 inches long—long enough to seat two students on one side—and 24 inches

wide. These may be used with chairs or stools. Each student needs a 24- to 30-inch-wide knee space. The legs at each end of resin-topped utility tables subtract about 6 inches from the width of the knee space under the table. The knee space of a 48-inch table will usually be only 36 inches wide, which is not sufficient for two students.

For durability, choose an oak-framed laboratory table with a resin top, available from most manufacturers. Sockets can be installed for laboratory apparatus. Check the connection between the leg and the table frame for durability, as the tables will be subject to a lot of abuse during their lifetime. Tables constructed with lag bolts may come apart when they are moved. A better design bolts the leg to a steel plate set into the frame. Stronger still is a design that bolts the leg to the plate using a bolt that passes completely through the leg and is held in place with a nut and washer. Any tables taller than 30 inches should be equipped with H-shaped stretchers that provide extra support for the legs.

"Through-bolt" table leg connection. (42)

The resin tops come in various colors. Lighter-colored tops may be considered more attractive, but they may be stained by some of the dyes used in biology classes.

Many teachers prefer to use a movable demonstration table, because they feel that a fixed table at the front of the room separates them

from the students and interferes with students' access to the board. A mobile teacher's table can have base cabinets or drawers, knee space, its own water and gas, and an electric cord, enabling it to be used nearly anywhere in the room.

Storage

It is desirable to provide base cabinets and countertops along at least two walls for storage and additional work space. All upper shelves and wall cabinets should have base cabinets beneath them, for safety reasons and as

Movable teacher's table. (43)

an ADA requirement. High-quality cabinets, such as those made of marine-grade plywood with plastic laminate fronts, should be a priority. Avoid particleboard assembly for casework, because this material is affected by moisture.

Every room should have several types of base cabinets. Consider units with drawers of various sizes, drawer and door units with adjustable shelves, and tote-tray cabinets that allow the teacher to store all of the items for an activity in one bin. Tote-tray cabinets are also useful for storing student kits, which can be brought out at laboratory time.

Wall cabinets are typically either 12 or 15 inches deep, and should be mounted about 18 inches above the countertop. Bookshelves should be at least 10 inches deep and should be adjustable to different heights.

Cabinets of various heights and depths will be needed for specialized storage of items such as rock and mineral samples for Earth science, and microscopes and glassware for biology and life science, as well as stands for aquariums, terrariums, and plants. Physical science makes extensive use of materials and equipment of varying sizes, types, and weights.

Rolling tote-tray storage unit. (44)

Allow space in the classroom for use of equipment such as laboratory carts, computer carts, a human skeleton on a stand with roll-

Flat-stock unit for posters and maps. (45)

ers, an animal cage, and a stream table. Teachers may choose to integrate recycling into classroom activities by including large storage bins with lids. It is also important to provide

storage for students' coats and book bags to keep these items out of the way during lab work.

Display Space

Chalkboards, marker boards, and tackboards are hung at roughly counter height, that is, 32 to 36 inches for students, and 36 inches for adults. Dry-erase marker boards are often used in place of chalkboards, because chalk dust can

Vertical dividers for storing flat objects. (46)

be harmful to both computers and people. However, there is also concern about the toxicity of permanent markers, and manufacturers' information should be studied. Sliding, multiple-panel boards can be used to extend a marker board without requiring more wall space.

The instructional focus area may support a variety of presentation formats, including video, laser disc, slides, projected microscope images, and overhead projection. Since a movable teacher's table is frequently used, controls, including light dimmers, may be installed in a wall panel that is easily accessible to the teacher.

Ceiling hooks or a 1-inch diameter steel pipe suspended from suitable structures, such as joists, above the ceiling tiles will provide a place to hang demonstration and experimental apparatus. Each hook should have at least a 50-pound capacity, and the pipe should hold

at least 200 pounds. It is advisable to overdesign the suspension system.

Utilities

All circuits or electrical outlets in the laboratory should have ground-fault interrupter (GFI) protection, to protect students against shocks. In order to avoid overloading circuits and eliminate the need for extension cords, overlapping wires, and plug-in outlet extenders, laboratories, classrooms, and preparation areas should be equipped with plenty of duplex electrical outlets. These should be available at frequent intervals along walls that have counters and cabinets. One duplex outlet for every two students at the laboratory stations is recommended. Four duplex outlets are desirable along the front or instructional area wall, and three on any wall that lacks cabinets. Computers require separate circuits. Wiring for network connections is also needed throughout the room.

DC power can be provided using small, dry cells such as 9-volt batteries (never automotive storage batteries). The teacher may use a portable unit that plugs into the AC outlet and is protected by a circuit breaker.

Providing outlets for electric power, cable television, and computer networking in an appropriate location will make it possible to connect an LCD projector or large-screen television for viewing Internet sites, videotapes, CD-ROMs, or images from a microscope.

It is never safe to run wires or conduits across a classroom floor in an attempt to for supply power for equipment that may be set up there. However, there are several ways to provide electric power to locations in the center of the room.

One example is pull-down, retractable electric cords, similar to those in automotive shops. These can be arranged as multiple outlets and equipped with computer network outlets. The primary drawbacks of this system are the dangling overhead wires and the tendency of the retractors to pull the cords back quickly, damaging ceiling tiles. Recessed floor outlets can bring utilities to the center of the room.

Care should be taken to investigate the characteristics with respect to safety of any alternative to wall outlets.

Two-way communication between the classroom and the office is essential.

Hot plates are often used in place of Bunsen burners, but they have the drawback that a student can get a bad burn from the hot surface even after power has been turned off. Hot plates draw a lot of electric current and can cause tripped circuit breakers, especially if the electricity supply is not adequate.

Science programs have been moving away from the use of gas at the middle school level. If gas is used, it should be located at the perimeter, near the sinks. The room should have a button-activated emergency shut-off valve. It is useful to have a central control valve that turns the gas on and off and that only the teacher can access.

Place emergency shut-off controls for water, electrical service, and gas near the teacher's station, not far from the door, and not too easily accessible to students.

Other utilities, such as a vacuum and deionized or distilled water are used so rarely at this level that the cost of installing a central system for any of them is usually prohibitive. Many

Recessed parabolic light fixture. (48)

Pendant, three-tube fluorescent light fixture. (49)

classrooms can share portable vacuum pumps. Remember to provide storage space for these units in a preparation or storage room. Distilled water can be purchased in bulk, or a small still can be set up in a preparation room. Water demineralizers or deionizers are available for mounting on the wall above a sink. Water containers are filled using a hose connected to the faucet.

Lighting and Darkening Rooms

General light levels of at least 50 foot-candles per square foot of floor surface are required for general classroom and laboratory work, and 75 to 100 foot-candles at the work surface. Because glare from direct light sources interferes with images on projector screens and computer monitors, parabolic fluorescent fixtures with grids that direct the light straight down have become standard in rooms that have computers.

Three-tube fixtures wired so that the middle tube is switched separately from the two outer tubes allow three levels of room lighting: three tubes lit, two tubes lit, and only one tube lit.

Providing separate switches for each row of lights allows additional options for room darkening. For example, when images are being projected onto a screen at the front of the room, just the front row of lights might be off.

Indirect lighting has been used successfully in rooms that have computers. In this type of fixture, the light shines onto the ceiling, bounces back, and is diffused throughout the room, providing strong lighting levels at the work surface without producing a bright light that reflects off computer screens. These fixtures can also be three-tube fixtures that operate as described above.

The increased use of LCD projectors, videocassette recorders, laser discs, and television images has complicated lighting design further. Projection screens tend to reflect all light, and a bright, overall illumination such as is produced by indirect fixtures will wash out the projected image. Providing recessed, dimmable, compact fluorescent light fixtures as supplemental lighting throughout the room allows the teacher to turn off the more intense general lighting, and the down-lights provide the necessary desktop illumination for note taking.

All of these lighting alternatives are more expensive than the traditional recessed, prismatic light troffer, but their use will become increasingly necessary over time.

A study of 100 fourth and fifth graders (Grocoff, 1996) concluded that skylights provide the most comfortable classroom lighting for students. The study tested fluorescent lights of various correlated color temperatures at two levels of illumination. The participants

Emergency gas shut-off button. (47)

6-8

ranked a general illumination of 50 foot-candles more comfortable than that of 100 foot-candles and reported various physical and behavioral symptoms when light at the extreme color ranges was used.

5000K lamps with parabolic lenses may be used to provide a warm color that is closest to daylight. 4100K lamps are acceptable substitutes.

The ability to darken the classroom includes the need to eliminate glare from sunlight, which, besides interfering with computer and projection use, hampers some investigations in physics, chemistry, and Earth science. For this purpose, one-inch miniblinds work well in general, but they are not sufficient for optics investigations that must be conducted in almost complete darkness.

Room-darkening shades are available that block almost all of the light from windows. They are made of a completely opaque material and have both edge and bottom tracks. Remember, too, that window-mounted ex-

Room-darkening shade. (50)

Rolling bulletin boards for darkening rooms. (51)

haust fans let sunlight in around their edges, and windows into preparation rooms or in the classroom doors are yet another source of light. Room-darkening shades are fairly expensive and are needed only when near-total darkness is required. If necessary, only one science room could be so equipped, in order to keep costs down. Rolling bulletin boards can be very effective for darkening rooms.

Computers

Space and GFI-protected electric power will be needed to accommodate several computers in each room. A class of 24 is likely to need at least six computer stations with connection points to the school's computer network. Each desktop computer station takes up 15 square feet, and a 20-amp GFI-protected electric circuit can service three computers. Surge protectors are also needed. Desktop computers may be kept on mobile carts or mounted permanently on low counters.

Computers mounted on rolling carts can be docked at a wall station or moved to any

location in the room. Plan to provide space for these computer carts next to various table arrangements. A docking space should allow the cart to be placed against the wall in a position suitable for computer use. The depth of this space should be roughly 5 feet, to accommodate the cart and allow 3 feet or more of clearance for a seated student. The aisle behind the student seating should be an additional 3 feet wide, to allow free movement.

A cart 21 inches deep and 30 inches wide will accommodate a standard desktop computer with a mouse and a pullout keyboard drawer. Carts with wider tops allow space for books and papers. Newer cart designs include a bracket beneath the top for a tower configuration.

Computer on a rolling cart at a workstation. (52)

Counters on which computers are to be installed permanently should be at table height and not higher than 32 inches, and there must be knee space beneath them. When power outlets are beneath the counter or when tower units are used, leave a 2-inch-diameter hole with a rubber grommet in the countertop for the wire connections. There are two reasons for not installing computers on countertops near sinks, the more obvious being that computers can be damaged by water. The other is that standard countertops are too high for comfortable computer use.

Although most classroom computers today are desktop units, laptop and notebook computers are becoming more powerful and less expensive, and may provide savings in the future. Some schools have installed laptop network connections at each workstation. When not in use, the laptops are kept in the equipment storage room, in cabinets that have power plugs for recharging the batteries. In order to be able to use the network, each laptop must have a network card, but this is not an expensive item. Investing in laptops eliminates the space needed for desktop computer stations and the cost of computer carts. A cabinet 30 inches wide, 15 inches deep, and 30 inches high can hold as many as 20 laptops. Eliminating six desktop computer stations can save almost 90 square feet of space. This represents significant savings in construction costs.

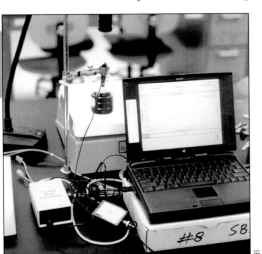

Laptop computer connected to a probe. (53)

Workstations for Students with Disabilities

An appropriate work area for students with physical disabilities includes a sink accessible to a person in a wheelchair. The *ADA Accessibility Guidelines for Buildings and Facilities* (ADAAG) specifies a number of requirements, including maximum counter heights, reach ranges, and grasping and twisting limitations. These specifications are for adults, but ADA recommendations are available for younger students.

For an adult, the top of a sink must not be mounted higher than 34 inches above the floor. Knee space at least 27 inches high and a minimum of 30 inches wide is required; by necessity, the sink depth will be no more than 6-1/2 inches. Resin sinks are generally not feasible in this

Wrist-blade faucet handles. (54)

situation, because of the requirements of the sink assembly. Controls for the faucet must also comply with the ADA guidelines, which require lever or wrist-blade faucet handles. At least one furniture manufacturer of utility islands produces a unit that meets ADAAG specifications.

Some schools use a mobile workstation. It can have a gas bottle and includes a water supply operated by an electric pump, an electrical power cord that is plugged into an out-

Mobile workstation for students with disabilities. (55)

let, and a holding tank for waste water that must be emptied regularly. It can be stationed anywhere and moved from room to room as needed. In order to make every room accessible, each room must have sufficient wall space, as well as cabinets and electrical outlets suitable for use with these mobile units.

Teacher's Space

Teachers need their own space for preparing lessons, making telephone calls, keeping essential papers and texts, and meeting with students. Some successful arrangements are

- a teacher's desk in an alcove in a laboratory/classroom
- an individual office in a preparation room, as described below
- a space between two laboratories
- an assigned space in a departmental office that has movable office partitions and a central meeting space for groups

When teaching is done in teams, using integrated curricula, the group office arrangement may work best. In this type of arrangement, provide distinct spaces for each teacher, a meeting area where the team can plan as a group with one or two students, and a storage area for shared equipment.

At a minimum, each teacher should have a desk area with an electrical outlet, computer network connection, telephone, file cabinet, and storage cabinet, all arranged to indicate that it is private and off-limits to students. The teacher's space should not be located in a classroom that is shared with other teachers.

Preparation and Storage Rooms

A preparation room is essential at the middle school level, and it is most convenient if it is next to, and accessible from, the laboratory/classroom. All doors to the room should lock. The room should be, at a minimum, 8 feet wide and 16 feet long, unless most equipment storage is in a separate storage room, in which case a length of 12 feet may be sufficient. A larger room located between two laboratory/classrooms can serve two teachers successfully.

The preparation room should have base and wall cabinets, tall storage units, shelves that are no higher than eye level, and counter space. Floor space for laboratory carts is also needed. There should be a sink with hot and cold water, and a drying rack is often required. This is also a good place for a spark-free refrigerator with an icemaker, a microwave, and a dishwasher. Gas may be needed, depending on the curriculum. For most middle school programs, a fume hood is needed in the preparation room.

A teacher's desk may be built into the

Teachers' office located between two laboratories.
(56)

counter space by installing a table-height 6-foot length of counter with knee space, adjacent file drawers, and a 2-inch-diameter hole at the back of the counter for the computer wiring. This desk should not be near the sink. Provide GFI-protected electric circuits, at least one computer network hookup, and a telephone.

Locating the room so that it gives teachers access without going through a classroom is desirable, because it allows teachers who share the room to work without disrupting classes in the adjacent space. A view window into the adjacent laboratory/classrooms enables teachers to observe any activity in those rooms and lets students know when the teachers are in their office.

Whether separate or combined preparation and equipment storage rooms will be needed depends on the science program. Storage should be for equipment only and must be supplemented by a chemical storage closet or room. A separate, secure chemical storage room may open off the preparation room.

Equipment storage rooms provide needed security and specialized storage for large, expensive, or sensitive equipment. Programs and enrollments change more often in middle schools than at other levels, so it is prudent to preserve as much flexibility as possible by installing tall wall cabinets, a variety of base cabinets, and open shelving. If the school curriculum integrates the sciences or offers alternating modules, centralized or movable storage units may be useful.

Hinged doors are preferable on the cabinets, because sliding doors waste about 3 inches of interior cabinet depth and can knock over bottles. Cabinets should have positive latches that can withstand seismic events without opening. Storage shelving of several depths is needed: 10 inches for books, 12 to 15 inches for multiple uses, and 18 to 24 inches for bulky items. It is best mounted on standards that allow adjustment to different heights. Some standards can lock in place for use in seismic areas.

A shallow drawer for storing poster board is very popular with middle school teachers. This flat-stock drawer will require a cabinet with at least a 30-inch-deep countertop. Cabinets that fit under 24- and 30-inch-deep counters have drawers that are only 21 and 27 inches deep, respectively. A cabinet with vertical dividers beneath a counter can store panels and other large, flat objects.

Rolling compact shelving units that require only one aisle for several banks of shelves are useful when space is at a premium and for schools where Earth, life, and physical sciences are integrated.

All chemicals should be kept in dedicated,

Rolling compact shelving. (57)

lockable, cabinets or separate chemical storage areas. Separate ventilation is needed for all rooms or closets in which chemicals are stored. Chemicals should never be stored in the classroom.

Chemicals must be divided into their compatible families, and incompatible chemicals are stored separately, at sufficient distance from each other. Secure, compact storage units for acids, flammables, and corrosives are available. Teachers should always use stock bottles and carry out preparations outside the student area.

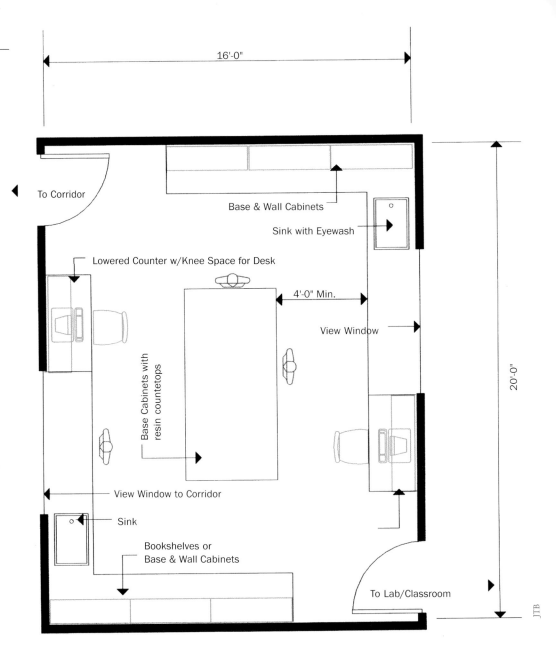

Figure 12.

Plan of a student project area.

Storage for hazardous materials. (58)

In general, one can never have sufficient storage. A critical inventory of all existing items can determine whether some items are no longer used and might be discarded. In case of a fire or accident, a complete list of what is stored, together with material safety data (MSDS) sheets will be needed.

Student Project Areas

With science curricula becoming more inquiry-oriented and more often directed toward individual and small-group work, there is an increasing need for space for long-term student projects. This space should be as close to the laboratory/classroom as possible. It is important to have a window between the two rooms or between the corridor and the student project room to facilitate supervision. A door from the corridor will allow students and teachers to use the project space without disrupting nearby classes.

Student project space has always been at a premium. One practical layout is to place base cabinets with countertops, wall cabinets, and at least two sinks with hot and cold water around the perimeter. A central-island work area made up of movable tables or additional base cabinets arranged back-to-back and covered with a resin countertop would make the space much more useful. Electric power with GFI-protected circuits and computer network connections should be installed along the perimeter and at the center island. Allow sufficient space between the perimeter counter and the center island so that students working at computer carts can access both work areas. The computer cart will require an aisle 4 or 5 feet wide.

Reference

Grocoff, Paul N. (1996). *Effects of Correlated Color Temperature on Perceived Visual Comfort*. Doctoral dissertation, University of Michigan, College of Architecture and Urban Planning. (Available from University Microfilms, 1-800-521-3042)

Student project area. (59)

Aquariums and terrariums for the observation, investigation, care, and cultivation of a variety of wildlife may be used as a design feature in the science area. Several new schools have large aquariums built into the walls of a student gathering space, where, in one instance, the aquarium is also visible from the adjacent laboratory/classroom. Terrariums can also be displayed in this manner.

A display has been developed consisting of an adjustable shelving system with one glass wall and various shelving and lighting options. If it is installed in a corridor wall outside a science room, students and teachers passing by can see the displays of plants, animals, specimens, rocks, or equipment and observe the activities in the room.

For further information:

ADA requirements .... Chapter 3

Safety, fume hoods .... Chapter 3
                         & Appendix B

Outdoor facilities .... Chapter 7

Finishing materials .... Chapter 8

Projectors, screens,
and other equipment .... Appendix D

8-9

CHAPTER 6

Designing Facilities for the High School (9–12)

A major principle of good science facilities planning is to avoid building for a single curricular model. Since continued change in educational trends is inevitable, any plans for science space should allow as much flexibility as possible in order to avoid the expense and considerable inconvenience of having to reconfigure the space at a later date.

Traditionally, the high school program, served by a fully-equipped wing of science rooms, has emphasized divisions between departments. In part because construction costs are reduced when water, gas, and special ventilation systems are concentrated in a single area, the departmentalized model for high schools has remained the norm.

But as schools have grown in recent years, educators have found that large class sizes are barriers to educational goals. Many high school programs have divided their large student bodies into smaller "houses" of 500 students or less. These operate as schools-within-the-school, with faculty teams teaching only the students in their own houses. Each house has its own classrooms for social studies, English, mathematics, and other subjects. Equipping each house with its own science area presents a considerable challenge to cost-conscious planning teams, since this normally requires that gas, water, and ventilation systems be replicated in several areas in the school.

One way schools have preserved the ability to use either departmentalized or "house" models, while keeping costs down and not sacrificing quality, is by placing their science facilities at the center of a "spoke" or pod configuration. This arrangement makes it possible to locate either the houses or the separate departments in each wing, with the science department clustered at the center. It also allows future staff to reorganize space in ways that continue to serve the needs of the student body.

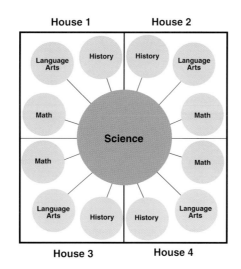

Figure 13.

Centralized science facilities in a "house" school.

Computers in the classroom. (60)

Grouping Facilities for Integration

Another important design consideration is clustering related facilities. Grouping science facilities together benefits both teaching and the sharing of equipment and resources. The trend toward integration with other subjects brings the additional advantage of coordinating related programs with portions of the sci-

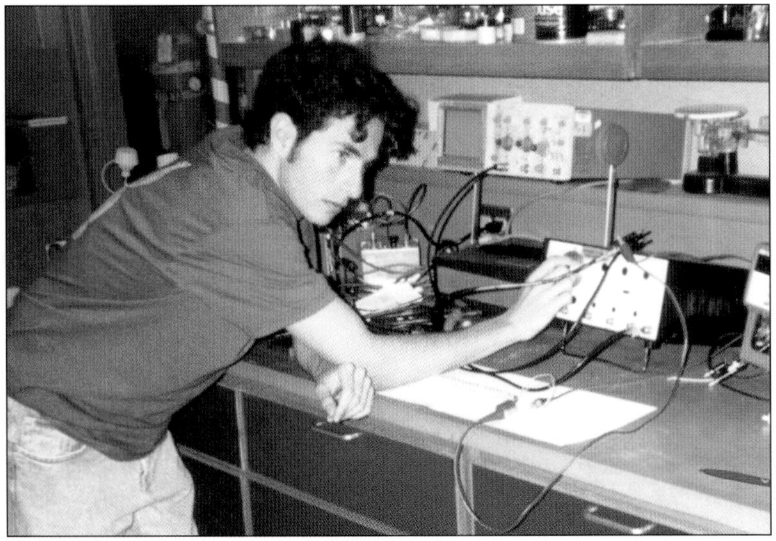

Jane B. Nelson

Technology lab. (61)

9–12

ence curriculum and energizing subjects such as mathematics and the applied sciences.

Increasingly, shop classrooms are being replaced by technology labs that use computer simulation to demonstrate scientific principles. These activities provide hands-on experiences that might not otherwise find a place in the science curriculum. If students recognize that these laboratories are teaching applied science, and if they are able to integrate their experiences with their understanding of science, they will have learned something of value. Locating the technology lab near the science wing can provide easy access for science teachers who want to illustrate an abstract concept with a quick but meaningful hands-on experience.

Locating a mathematics classroom close to the science area is an advantage to the science program because mathematics is used throughout science. In addition, the mathematics program benefits, because newer models for teaching mathematics emphasize hands-on applications, and space in the mathematics room is often insufficient for these experiences. Projects that combine the two disciplines can be housed in the science department's student project area.

Today's media laboratories make use of applied sciences, and they should also have easy access to the science space. Student teams can develop and produce media programs, using equipment and resources from the science area and technology from the media center. An imaginatively designed space may serve as the site for programs students broadcast to the rest of the school and beyond.

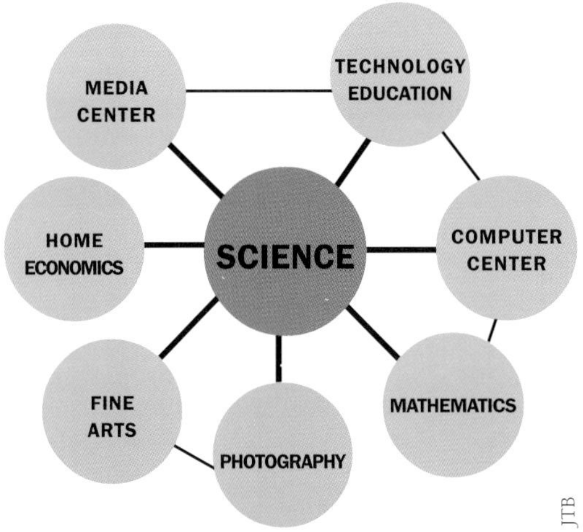

JTB

Figure 14.

Recommended adjacencies.

Finally, if consumer science, formerly known as home economics, is adjacent to the science area, joint projects and investigations in the life sciences can be carried out in either space.

Types of Science Rooms

In high school, science rooms are almost always specially designed, separate teaching spaces. As in the middle school, the increasing integration of science curricula makes it even more important to ensure that the school's facilities do not limit the types of subjects and strategies that can be used. Given sufficient space, flexible furniture arrangements, and appropriate equipment, almost any type of science instruction can be possible in most spaces.

Some schools have designed generic laboratories that, with few exceptions, have everything necessary for any science course. This approach has the advantage of allowing curricular changes and future enrollment growth that may require changes in the allocation of space. Placing extra conduits for utilities in the floors and walls during construction is an easy way to provide additional flexibility for expansion and future improvements.

The two most commonly used models for science rooms are (1) separate laboratory and classroom space, and (2) combination laboratory/classrooms. While an effective science room today is generally expected to accommodate work in all science disciplines, additional laboratories may be desired for specialized or advanced courses that require special equipment, fixtures, ventilation, or other resources.

Space Requirements

Class size is an important design factor, because it helps determine the amount of space and number of workstations that will be needed. To accommodate current technology needs and teaching practices, a good science room will generally require

- a minimum of 45 square feet per student for a stand-alone laboratory, 1,080 square feet for a class of 24 students
- a minimum of 60 square feet per student for a combination laboratory/classroom, 1,440 square feet for a class of 24 students

The 1990 NSTA position statement on laboratory science recommends a maximum class size of 24 students in high school.

An additional space of 15 square feet is needed for each computer station and 20 square feet for a workstation to accommodate a student with disabilities. At least 10 square feet per student is needed for teacher preparation space and storage space. Space is also needed for longer-term student projects.

A ceiling height of 10 feet is desirable for a science room. This is particularly important for classes in physics, where some investigations may require a high ceiling, and in chemistry, where an investigation may produce clouds of smoke. Using a projection screen that is 6 x 8 feet won't work well in a room with ceiling less than 9 feet high, because tables and desks will block the lower portions of the screen. Under no circumstances should a classroom ceiling be lower than 8 feet.

For safety and flexibility, a rectangular room at least 30 feet wide, without alcoves, is recommended. The room should have at least two exits and doorways that accommodate students with physical disabilities.

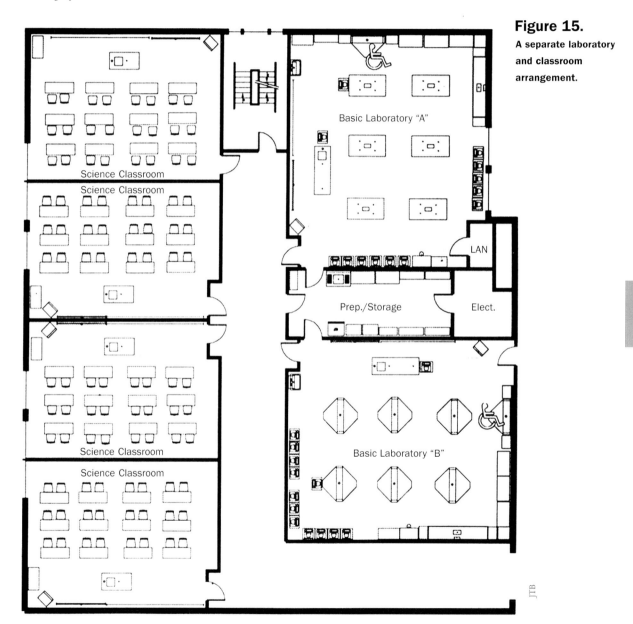

Figure 15.
A separate laboratory and classroom arrangement.

Science Classroom

Science Classroom

Science Classroom

Science Classroom

Basic Laboratory "A"

Basic Laboratory "B"

Prep./Storage

Elect.

LAN

9-12

Shared laboratory with two adjacent classrooms and folding partitions. (62)

Fanning Howey Assoc.

Separate Laboratories and Classrooms

Science curricula require both laboratory and classroom space. In some cases, to reduce the number of laboratories necessary and thus to save on costs, two teachers may share a laboratory but have their own "home" classrooms. Sharing may also be accomplished using a classroom-laboratory-classroom arrangement with movable partitions separating the three spaces. Because laboratory space is approximately twice as expensive to build and equip as classroom space, constructing two classrooms for each laboratory reduces costs significantly.

But there are several caveats to keep in mind when considering building one laboratory for two classrooms.

• Scheduling the use of the common labora-

tory can be tricky and requires close cooperation and planning between the teachers sharing the space.

• Science based on inquiry relies more on laboratory and field experiences than traditional instruction does. Good science instruction is no longer divided into lectures and laboratories, and many lessons involve a mixture of classroom and laboratory work.

• Thorough discussions in science call for small, frequent hand-on activities. Having to postpone a hands-on illustration of a key idea, a lecture on safety, or a discussion of a concept until a laboratory is available is a real loss.

• School administrators, under pressure of overenrollment and overcrowding, may consider the shared laboratory an available teaching space and, in spite of all the good

A generic four-student workstation. (63)

JTB

intentions at the time of design and construction, schedule non-science classes in it. Unfortunately, this happens often, and it defeats the very purpose of the shared space concept.

• Movable partitions that act as satisfactory sound barriers between adjacent spaces are heavy and expensive. When open, they take up wall and floor space that might be put to better use in another program activity. The partitions are also more easily damaged than block walls.

The general requirements for a separate laboratory are similar to those of a combination laboratory/classroom.

The Combination Laboratory/Classroom

The combination classroom and laboratory requires a larger room, but it has several advantages over a stand-alone laboratory, including providing maximum instructional options and the most flexible use of space.

The two most popular arrangements are

(1) a room with fixed student workstations and a separate section for classroom instruction, and

(2) A room that has a flexible arrangement, with utilities at the perimeter and movable tables that can form various configurations for laboratory and classroom work.

When designing either kind of room, three key principles of room layout should be observed:

• All students face the teacher when they are in the classroom area.

9-12

- Sufficient classroom space is allotted to the students so that they can work safely.
- During laboratory activities, the teacher can supervise the students easily and movement around the room is unimpeded. Paths for egress are a vital safety factor and must be kept clear at all times.

In all room arrangements, there should be a minimum of 4 feet between the perimeter counters and the areas for general and group seating, and at least 4 feet around each grouping of tables. In classroom format, provide a minimum of 8 feet from the front wall of the classroom to the first tables. The teacher then will be able to move around easily, and have use of a table and equipment such as a projector.

A Classroom Area and Fixed Workstations

Laboratory areas with fixed student workstations allow the teacher to supervise and assist students with ease. Freestanding utility islands may serve as complete workstations for four or more students. If the room is large, the islands may be installed at one end of the room.

Universal laboratory station. (64)

An alternative is a utility island that provides power and utilities to movable laboratory tables that serve as the primary work surfaces when pulled up to the utilities. The latter arrangement permits more flexible use of space.

Installed workstations should always allow an aisle space of at least 4 feet between the perimeter cabinets and the rows of students.

Trifacial utility island with tables drawn up to three sides. (65)

The trifacial utility island. A popular design for fixed stations is the trifacial utility island (triple table hub). Movable tables are drawn up to the three longer sides of these six-sided islands, creating work areas for students who share large, deep sinks that they access from the three narrower sides. Gas, electrical outlets, and computer data wiring can be installed at the three longer sides, adjacent to the tables. Each trifacial island can accommodate three large tables (48 by 54 inches) or six small tables (21 or 24 by 54 inches), and thus provide laboratory work space for 12 students.

The tables may be combined and rearranged as necessary to permit activities re-

quired in the various disciplines. Tables are available that have electrical "pigtails" and outlets that plug into the hub units, providing power and data wiring to the far end of the table for computers and other electrical equipment.

Octagonal and rectangular islands. Fixed octagonal workstations with trough sinks and water supplies at each end work well in all disciplines, provided there are trough covers for the sinks, to create the long, flat surface often needed in physics.

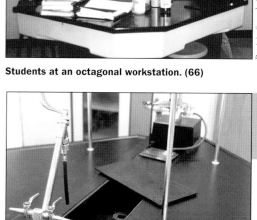

Students at an octagonal workstation. (66)

Fixed rectangular stations with central sinks can be modified to provide a 6-foot-long work surface, but these sinks are harder to cover, because the faucets are in the center of the table. Both types of workstations can be equipped with sockets for apparatus rods, if desired, and outlets for computer network connections. Various storage compartments for supplies and equipment can be installed beneath the counters of these stations.

Classroom section. The classroom portion of

Octagonal workstation with trough sink with cover. (67)

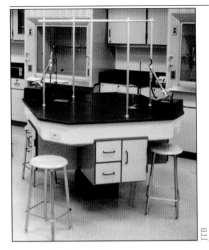

An octagonal workstation with below-counter storage units. (68)

the room should be as flexible as possible and provide various arrangements for student seating. Desk and chair combinations, tablet arm chairs, or tables with chairs may be used. The laboratory tables from the trifacial units may be rearranged for the classroom seating, but moving the tables takes some time.

A Flexible Room Arrangement

In the flexible laboratory/classroom, sinks and utilities are located on perimeter counters, and students use movable, flat-topped laboratory tables for both classroom and laboratory activities. This design makes the most efficient use of space and renders the room adaptable to a wide variety of uses. The flexible room is also more easily modified than a laboratory/classroom with fixed workstations or service islands.

Flat-topped tables used as student workstations allow multiple arrangements and combinations for laboratory work and small-group activities that would not be possible with desks with sloping tops.

Two tables, each seating two students on a side, form a

Flat-topped movable tables and perimeter sinks. (69)

workstation when placed together against a counter, with the longer table sides perpendicular to the counter. Each group of four stu-

Flat-topped tables drawn up to perimeter sinks. (70)

Flat-topped tables set up for lab work. (71)

dents has use of a sink, a source of heat , such as gas or hot plate, electric power for equipment and computers, and, often, network connections. The sinks should be installed in such a way that when tables are drawn up to the counters there will be enough space be-

tween the tables for students to access the sinks easily. Gas jets, if used, are between the sinks.

A surface-mounted "raceway" may be installed above the counter's backsplash to bring in electric power and data outlets at regular intervals along the counter.

Furnishings

The following describes the needs of a flexible laboratory/classroom with movable tables and perimeter counters, sinks, and utilities. The text also applies to laboratories and laboratory/classrooms with fixed workstations.

Sinks

Sinks for student investigations should be fairly wide and deep and have swiveling, gooseneck faucets that allow students to fill and clean large containers. A good rule of thumb is to provide one sink for four students. Resin sinks are recommended, because they resist chemical corrosion; however, stainless-steel sinks may be an acceptable money-saving alternative in a room that is used only for programs such as physics, where the use of corrosive chemicals is minimal. Several sinks should be equipped with dual eyewashes.

All sinks should have hot and cold water.

Deep perimeter sink with a swivel faucet. (72)

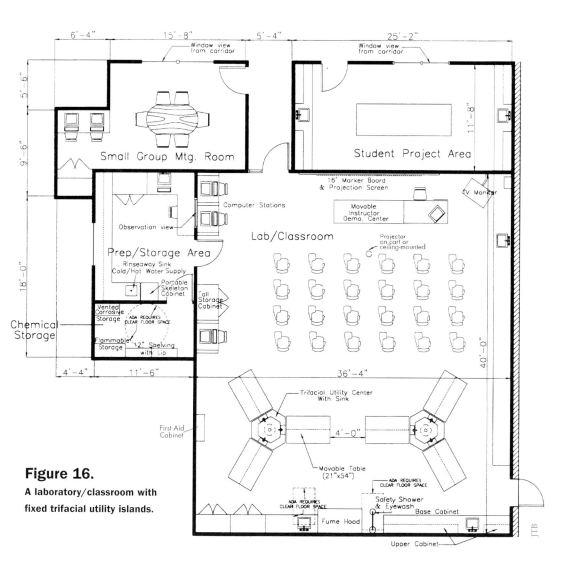

Figure 16.

A laboratory/classroom with fixed trifacial utility islands.

Labels in figure:
6'-4" · 15'-8" · 5'-4" · 25'-2"
Window view from corridor
Window view from corridor
Small Group Mtg. Room
Student Project Area
16' Marker Board & Projection Screen
TV Monitor
Computer Stations
Movable Instructor Demo. Center
Observation view
Lab/Classroom
Prep/Storage Area
Projector on cart or ceiling-mounted
Rinseaway Sink Cold/Hot Water Supply
Portable Skeleton Cabinet
Tall Storage Cabinet
Vented Corrosive Storage
ADA REQUIRES CLEAR FLOOR SPACE
Chemical Storage
Flammable Storage
12" Shelving with Lip
4'-4" · 11'-6"
36'-4"
40'-0"
18'-0"
9'-6"
5'-6"
Trifacial Utility Center With Sink
4'-0"
First Aid Cabinet
Movable Table (21"x54")
ADA REQUIRES CLEAR FLOOR SPACE
ADA REQUIRES CLEAR FLOOR SPACE
Safety Shower & Eyewash
Base Cabinet
Fume Hood
Upper Cabinet

Acid dilution trap installed beneath a sink. (73)

Serrated nozzle with a hose. (74)

tem. A more effective but also more expensive method of dealing with corrosive wastes is with an acid-resistant piping system and central acid dilution tank.

Faucets should be equipped with aerators. Serrated nozzles adapted for the attachment of hoses are an option, but they increase the pressure of the water, causing splattering. Some of these can be unscrewed, but teachers often respond by attaching a length of rubber hose to them to alleviate the problem.

It is also an advantage to have a large, deep sink with hot and cold water and adjacent counter space for various purposes, such as cleaning large containers. Two very convenient specialty sinks to consider for the laboratory are

- a "rinseaway" sink, which has a 6- to 10-foot-long molded fiberglass tray with raised edges that slopes down to a sink basin, facilitating the cleanup of plant and animal specimens and messy items. This tray accommodates experiments that need running water and a drain, and require long-term storage. The sink may be equipped with a garbage disposal or a plaster trap to catch sand or gravel. A pullout eyewash sprayer on a hose is useful both for safety

The "rinseaway" sink. (75)

This minimizes the need for separate heating facilities in many investigations and improves student hygiene. Schools need to be mindful of the maximum temperature of the hot water and keep it safely below the scalding point.

Check state and local regulations for hazardous materials to see if special installations will be needed. If the program calls for corrosive chemicals, supply the teacher's sink with an acid dilution trap. This trap is filled with limestone chips that neutralize the acid before it enters the regular waste-piping sys-

9-12

The "slop" sink. (76)

and cleaning up at the sink, but it cannot substitute for a dual eyewash.

- a deep, enameled-porcelain, wall-mounted janitor's slop sink, which is very useful for cleaning large containers and filling deep vessels with water. Avoid the typical fixed faucet and opt for a swiveling, gooseneck one, because the fixed faucet reduces the open area of the bowl.

Glassware drying racks come in various sizes, and are often useful if installed above some or all of the perimeter sinks. Mount each rack so that it drains directly into the sink rather than down the wall. Request a high backsplash, because the drying rack must be mounted high enough to clear the faucet. Some teachers find the fixed drying rack a waste of space and prefer a standard kitchen-counter drying rack, which can be removed and stored beneath the sink when not in use.

Work Space

For work space, counters 36 inches high and tables 30 inches high are convenient for most students. Countertops should be at least 24 inches deep. A counter depth of 30 inches will provide increased work space. Chairs or stools may be used for seating, but tall stools are not advisable, for safety reasons.

Countertops should be made of resin or a similar chemical-resistant material. They need to be caulked between the backsplash and the wall, and along any other joints, using clear silicone. Backsplashes 4 inches high are standard. They should also run along the counter beside any tall cabinets, all fume hoods, and other surfaces that interrupt or are set into the countertop. Near water sources, always

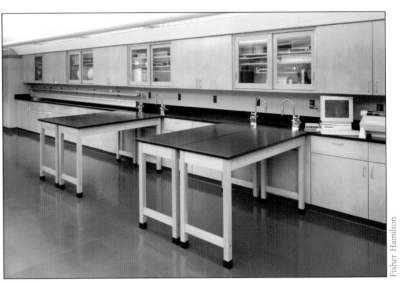

A laboratory/classroom with perimeter countertops and movable tables. (77)

use one-piece countertops with backsplashes and no seams.

Flat-topped, movable tables, 24 by 54 inches, and 30 inches high can be used for both classroom and laboratory work and may be pushed together to form larger surfaces. The tables should be large enough so two students can sit on one side. Allow at least 8 inches between the bottom of the table and the chair seat. Each student needs a knee space 24 inches wide, or as close to it as possible. Most 48-inch-long resin-topped utility tables have knee space only 36 inches wide—not wide enough for two—because the legs at each end reduce the amount of space under the table.

These tables should have tops made of resin, or a similar material, and may be equipped with sockets for apparatus rods.

For durability, the best choice is an oak-

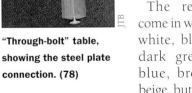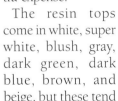

"Through-bolt" table, showing the steel plate connection. (78)

framed utility table with a resin top. The connection between the leg and table frame is critical for the durability of these otherwise sturdy tables. Many manufacturers lag-bolt the leg to the frame, which often produces failures when the tables are moved around, because the leg acts as a lever and pulls the bolt out. A better design bolts the leg to a steel plate set into the frame. In the strongest design, a bolt passing through the plate and leg is held in place with a nut and a washer. Since these tables will be subject to a lot of abuse during their lifetime, the strongest table is worth the extra expense.

The resin tops come in white, super white, blush, gray, dark green, dark blue, brown, and beige, but these tend to be about 20 percent more expensive than black. The lighter colors may brighten a dark room, but they are subject to discoloration by some of the dyes used in secondary courses.

Casework manufacturers have introduced tops made of marble-like products similar to those used for kitchen countertops and vanities. These materials are expensive and may be stained by classroom chemicals; they do not have the history of proven chemical resistance that resin has.

Many teachers prefer to use a movable table, because they feel that a fixed table at the front of the room separates them from the students and interferes with students' access to the board. A mobile teacher's table can have base cabinets, drawers, knee space, and its own water, gas, and electrical service.

Movable teacher's table. (79)

For safety reasons, workstations for chemistry classes and in specialized chemistry laboratories should be at standing height and all stools and chairs should be removed. Biology classes require seating for microscope work.

Physics teachers need a clear work surface at least 6 feet long for equipment such as air tracks. Many standard designs for science casework are shorter than 6 feet, so non-standard casework should be specified as needed.

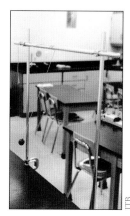

C-clamp. (80)

Physics teachers also like long, flat tables with apparatus rods clamped to the edges or fitted into sockets recessed into the top. "C-clamp" apparatus rods have limited clamp depth and can be used only with tabletops that are no more than 1¼ inches thick. Fixed rod sockets should be specified only in cases where they are essential, because they limit flexibility and interrupt the

Typical physics laboratory/classroom, with C-clamps on a flat-topped table. (81)

smooth surface of the tabletop, making it difficult for students to take notes.

Laboratory/classrooms specific to physics require less perimeter casework and fewer sinks than comparable rooms for biology or chemistry; one sink may suffice for the class. Movable tables serve well for lectures and experiments in physics rooms, provided that

An arrangement of flat-topped tables. (82)

sufficient space is available for their use in various configurations.

Storage

It is desirable to provide base cabinets and countertops along at least two walls for storage and additional work space. High-quality cabinets, such as those made of marine-grade plywood with plastic laminate fronts, should be a priority. Avoid particleboard assembly for casework, because this material is affected by moisture.

Every room needs several types of base cabinets. Consider units with drawers of various sizes, drawer and door units with adjustable shelves, and tote-tray cabinets that allow the teacher to store all of the items for a class or activity in one bin. Tote-tray cabinets are also useful for storing student laboratory kits that can be brought out at laboratory time and for setting aside make-up work.

Pull-down, overhead electrical cord. (83)

Power poles carrying electrical and data wires from the ceiling to the computer. (84)

Wall cabinets are typically either 12 or 15 inches deep, and should be mounted about 18 inches above the countertop. Bookshelves should be at least 10 inches deep and adjustable to different heights.

Cabinets of various heights and depths will be needed for specialized storage of items such as rock and mineral samples for Earth science; a skeleton on a rolling stand, microscopes, and glassware for biology and life science; and stands for aquariums, terrariums, and plants. Physical science makes extensive use of materials and equipment of varying sizes, types, and weights.

Allow floor space in the classroom for use of equipment such as laboratory carts, computer carts, an animal cage, and a stream table. It is also important to provide storage for students' coats and book bags to keep these items out of the way during lab work.

Display Space

Chalkboards, marker boards, and tackboards are hung at roughly counter height. Dry-erase marker boards are often used in place of chalkboards because chalk dust can be harmful both to computers and people. However, there is also concern about the toxicity of the permanent markers, and manufacturers' information should be studied. Sliding, multiple-panel boards can be used to extend a marker board without requiring more wall space.

The instructional focus area may support a variety of presentation formats, including video, laser disc, slides, projected microscope images, and overhead projection. Since a movable teacher's demonstration table is frequently used, controls, including light dim-

mers, may be installed in a wall panel that is easily accessible to the teacher.

Provision should be made for suspending objects from the ceiling. Tracks with sliding hooks can replace the standard "T-bar" grid of pipes and provide a variety of places for hanging various teaching aids and models. The suspension system for this grid must be much stronger than the typical ceiling grid. A less sophisticated solution is to suspend several 1-inch-diameter steel pipes beneath the ceiling using standard pipe clamps, and then to tie or clamp the items to these pipes. The pipes must be suspended from a suitable structure, such as joists from the floor above. The hooks should have at least a 50-pound capacity, and each pipe should hold at least 200 pounds. It is advisable to over-design the suspension system.

Utilities

Classrooms will need plenty of duplex electrical outlets carrying standard household current on separate circuits to avoid overload, all with ground-fault interrupters (GFI) for safety. Analyze the equipment that will be used in order to determine if any higher voltages are needed. DC power can be provided by small cells, not automotive storage batteries, or by portable units that plug into AC outlets and are protected by circuit breakers.

To ensure future flexibility for the science program, all classrooms built today should have wiring with multiple outlets for voice, video, and data network connections. Many schools are using fiberoptic cable for long hallway runs, but most still use copper wire in classrooms. Two-way voice communication between every classroom and the office is essential.

Science rooms need power and data lines at each student workstation. It is never safe to run wires or conduits across a classroom floor to provide power to workstations or equipment in the center of the room. However, there are several ways to provide electric power to these locations. These include:

- Pull-down electric cords, similar to those in automotive shops. These can be arranged as multiple outlets and equipped with computer network outlets. The primary drawbacks of this system are the dangling overhead wires and the tendency of the retractors to pull the cords back quickly, damaging ceiling tiles.

- Power poles, like those that are popular in open offices. These provide a more permanent arrangement. Again, both electric and computer network wiring can be delivered anywhere in the space, fed from the ceiling. The primary drawbacks of this system are a lack of flexibility because the poles cannot be moved easily and the relatively fragile nature of the pole systems, which are not designed for the type of abuse possible in a classroom.

- Recessed floor boxes that have lids with rotating "wire-management blocks" that open to allow wires to pass through and close when not in use. These boxes contain several power and network-connection outlets. The electrical outlets in the boxes should be raised above the bottom of the floor box to provide additional protection from any spills in that area of the floor. A model is available that holds the outlets vertically, away from the opening of the floor box. Floor boxes should not be located near safety showers or in areas where water and chemicals are used.

Do not use the old "tombstone"-type floor outlets that are fixed and stick up above the floor, because these are tripping hazards and greatly reduce the flexibility of the room. Also avoid floor outlets that are flush with the floor or that have hinged brass cover plates that may break off easily, exposing the outlet to dirt and spills.

Extra care should be taken to investigate the pros and cons with respect to safety of each alternative, especially the floor boxes, and to ensure that everyone, including the custodial staff, is informed of procedures for the safe use of the floor boxes.

The Orlando Science Center in Florida has flexible exhibition space with columns that carry electric power, computer networks, water, sewage, and gas. If a particular display needs any of these utilities, connections are close at hand and can be made easily and with little expense.

Today, gas is used less often than in the past because it is expensive and requires particular caution and diligence. It is primarily used in chemistry. If the science program requires its use, gas should be installed at the perimeter, near

Emergency gas shutoff. (85)

the sinks. When gas is provided by a central system, an emergency shut-off valve, activated by pushing a highly visible button, will be needed. A central control valve that enables the teacher to shut off the gas in the room as needed is useful.

Emergency shut-off controls for water, electrical service, and gas should be near the teacher's station, not far from the door, and not easily accessible to students.

Distilled water is used almost daily in high school science, and most schools build in their own still system. Remember to provide storage space for these units in a preparation or storage room. If space is not available, distilled water can be purchased in bulk, but the ultimate cost and storage requirements may make the still system more attractive. Water demineralizers or deionizers can be mounted on the wall above a sink, so that containers can be filled through a flexible hose connected to the faucet. High school classes generally need vacuums, and portable vacuum pumps may be the best option for this. Whether it is built in or not, this equipment requires specialized storage.

Fume hoods are used in certain physical science, chemistry, and life science classes, and are required in laboratories where hazardous or vaporous chemicals are used.

Lighting and Darkening Rooms

Classroom lighting has become a more difficult design problem because of the rapid increase in the use of computers, cable TV, and LCD projectors. Light levels of at least 50 foot candles for the general classroom and 75 to 100 foot-candles at the work surface are required for general classroom and laboratory work, but computer screens and projection screens do not perform well in the glare from direct light sources. Parabolic fluorescent fixtures with grids that direct light straight down have become standard in rooms that have computers. Three-tube fixtures with the middle tube switched separately from the outer tubes allow four levels of lighting: all three tubes, two tubes, one tube, or no tubes lit. Separate switches for each row of lights provide flexibility in room darkening. For example, when images are being projected onto a screen at the front of the room, the front row of lights can be turned off, the middle of the room may have only one tube lit, and the rear may have two tubes lit.

Indirect lighting has also been used successfully in rooms with computers. With this type of fixture, the light bounces off the ceiling and is diffused around the room, providing strong lighting levels at the work surface without producing a bright visible light source that would reflect off computer screens. These fixtures are also available as three-tube fixtures and can be operated as described above.

The increased use of videotapes, laser discs, television, and images projected onto large screens from LCD projectors has complicated lighting design still further. Projection screens tend to reflect all of the light that shines onto them, and bright, overall illumination will "wash out" the desired image.

Providing recessed, dimmable, compact fluorescent light fixtures as supplemental lighting throughout the room allows the teacher to turn off the more intense general lighting. The downlights provide the necessary desktop illumination for note-taking without washing out the image on the projection screen.

All of these lighting solutions are more ex-

Recessed parabolic fluorescent lighting fixture. (86)

9-12

One-inch mini-blinds can provide room-darkening for some rooms. (87)

Fisher Hamilton

pensive than the traditional recessed, prismatic light troffer, but they should be considered when designing the laboratory/classroom of the future.

The ability to darken the classroom is very important, because daylight coming through the windows creates glare on computer screens, washes out images on the projection screen and hampers certain investigations in physics, chemistry, life science, and Earth science. One-inch miniblinds work well in most rooms, but they are not sufficient for optics experiments that need almost complete darkness. They are also easily damaged. Room-darkening shades that slide into side and bottom tracks and are made from totally opaque material block out most of the light from windows. These shades are fairly expensive, and they should be considered only when almost complete darkness is needed. Several new schools have used sliding bulletin boards to darken windows and provide extra display space at the same time.

Remember that when exhaust fans replace windowpanes, they let light in around their edges and through the dampers. Windows into preparation rooms and windows in doors also admit light into the classroom. Solutions need to be found for these problem areas as well.

Computers

The use of the computer in the high school science classroom is growing. It is advisable to provide space and GFI-protected electrical power for as many computers as possible in a room. In designing new construction, one duplex power and data outlet for every four students is a good ratio to use. A class of 24 students will need at least six computer dock-

Most computers today are large desktop units. (88)

ing stations, with connection points to the school's and the district's computer network. Provide one dedicated 20-amp duplex electrical circuit for every three computers. A desktop computer station, whether mounted on a

Two different styles of computer cart. (89) & (90)

JTB

cart or permanently mounted on a counter, takes up about 15 square feet of space.

The location of computer stations will depend on the nature of the classroom. Computers should be stationed as far away from chalkboards and sources of water as possible. Desktop computers are often mounted on rolling carts that can be docked at wall stations or moved to any part of the room. To accommodate a standard desktop computer, the cart should be at least 21 inches deep and 30 inches wide, and should have a pullout keyboard drawer with space for the use of a mouse. Wider carts provide space for books and papers. Newer designs have a bracket beneath the top to accommodate a tower unit. Students should be able to use the computers while the carts are docked at wall stations.

When planning space for the computer carts next to various table configurations, allow space for the length of the cart, seating at the cart, and clear passage behind the seating. The depth of the docking space should be roughly 5 feet, to accommodate the cart and allow 3 feet or more of clearance for a seated student. The aisle behind the seated

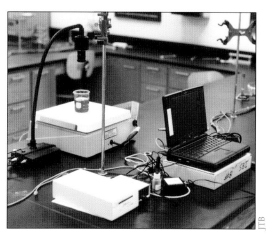
A laptop computer connected to a local network. (91)

student should be at least 5 feet wide, to allow free movement behind the cart..

If computers are to be installed at permanent locations, provide counter space at table height, and no higher than 32 inches, with knee space beneath. If the power outlet is beneath the counter or a tower unit is being used, leave a 2-inch-diameter hole with a rubber grommet in the countertop for the wire connections. Do not mount computers near sinks, for two reasons, the more obvious being that computers can be damaged by water. The other is that standard countertops are too high for comfortable computer use.

In response to continued reductions in the prices of laptop computers, many schools are moving toward their use, installing the appropriate wiring and connecting them to the network. The laptops can be locked in the storage room for security and recharging and to avoid the risk of accidental exposure to water or chemicals during laboratory investigations. These laptops will need network cards recog-

nized by the school's file server. The room would also benefit from having a high-speed printer for producing student reports using the laptops. Since it is inevitable that students will try to print out their work five minutes before the bell, the classroom printer will require both speed and a large memory.

Workstations for Students with Disabilities

A work area for students with physical disabilities includes a sink and utilities accessible to a person in a wheelchair. The Americans with Disabilities Act (ADA) requires that at least one sink in each laboratory be in compliance with its guidelines. Controls for the faucet usually have lever, or "wrist blade," handles. The regulations prescribe a maximum sink height and minimum clearance below the sink for the seated student. It is

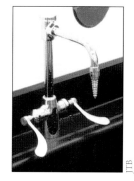
Wrist-blade handle. (92)

difficult to meet these requirements with a resin sink attached to the bottom of a resin countertop, because the cross-supports beneath the sink reduce the space available for the sink assembly.

Some schools use a mobile workstation. It has bottled gas, a water supply operated by an electric pump, an electrical power cord, and a holding tank for waste water that must be emptied regularly. This unit can be stationed anywhere and moved from room to room as

needed. In order to make every room accessible, each room must have sufficient wall space, as well as cabinets and electrical outlets suitable for use with these mobile units.

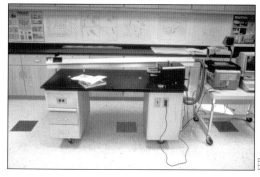
A mobile workstation for a disabled student. (93)

Teacher's Space

Teachers need their own space for preparing their lessons, making telephone calls, keeping essential papers and texts, and meeting with students. There are a number of successful arrangements:

- a teacher's desk in an alcove in a laboratory/classroom
- an individual office in a preparation room, as described below
- an assigned space in a departmental office that has movable office partitions and a central meeting space for groups

Combination faculty/departmental office. (94)

At a minimum, teachers should have their own desk areas, each with a computer, network connection, telephone, file cabinet, and storage cabinet, arranged to indicate that it is private and off-limits to students. The teacher's space

Teacher's office. (95)

A view window into a classroom. (96)

should not be located in a classroom that is shared with other teachers and should never be in a chemical storage room.

Preparation and Storage Rooms

Preparation space for the teacher is essential at the high school level, because the use of stock bottles and hazardous source materials in the classroom is never recommended.

The preparation room should be next to, and accessible from, the laboratory/classroom. All doors to the room should have locks. Access to the corridor is desirable, as it will allow the teacher to use the preparation room without disturbing a class in the next room. A view window into the laboratory/classroom facilitates supervision of students and lets students know when the teacher is in the office. Storage in a combined preparation/storage room should be for equipment and must be supplemented by a separate, locked chemical storage room or closet. A separate and secure chemical storage room may open off the preparation room.

The preparation room should be at least 8 feet wide and 16 feet long. If most storage is in another room, a preparation room 12 feet long may be sufficient. A larger room located between two laboratory/classrooms can successfully serve two teachers.

The room should have base and wall cabinets, tall storage units, 12-inch bookshelves, and counter space. Allow floor space for laboratory carts and space for desired equipment, such as a distillation unit or an autoclave. A sink with hot and cold water is needed and,

A teacher's room located between two laboratory/classrooms. (97)

frequently, a drying rack. A teacher's desk may be built into the counter space by installing a 6-foot length of counter at table height, with knee space, adjacent file drawers, and a 2-inch-diameter hole at the back of the counter for the computer wiring. This desk should not be near the sink. The preparation room is also a good place for a dishwasher, a microwave, and a spark-free laboratory refrigerator with an icemaker. Provide separate electric circuits with GFI-protected outlets, at least one computer network data hookup, and a telephone. Gas may be needed, depending on the curriculum. A fume hood is also needed for most programs.

Storage rooms provide needed security and specialized storage for large, expensive, or sensitive equipment. When planning a storage room, provide base cabinets of various types, wall cabinets, tall cabinets, and flexible, open shelving. Consider a variety of base cabinets with drawers of different sizes, drawer and door units, and adjustable shelves. Tote-tray cabinets are frequently included. If the school curriculum integrates the sciences or offers alternating modules, centralized or movable

9-12

storage units may be useful.

Hinged doors on wall cabinets are recommended, because sliding doors waste about 3 inches of interior cabinet depth, and the slides tend to become corroded when the cabi-

Flat-stock drawer unit. (98)

nets store chemicals. Wall cabinets 7 feet tall can accommodate models and other large lightweight objects.

Large paper items, such as maps or poster board, can be stored in a shallow drawer. This flat-stock drawer requires a base cabinet with a countertop at least 30 inches deep, because cabinets that fit under 24- and 30-inch-deep counters have drawers that are only 21 and 27 inches deep, respectively. Drawers with a width of 35 to 36 inches will accommodate most posters. Vertical dividers beneath a counter can store panels and other large, flat objects.

The storage system should have provision for labels on the outside of the cabinets. Many teachers prefer glass doors on cabinets that are used for equipment, in spite of their expense and fragility, because it is easier to find

Vertical dividers below a counter for storing large, flat items. (99)

materials in them. However, these qualities can also make the cabinets a housekeeping and security problem.

Storage shelving comes in several depths: 10 inches for books, 12 to 15 inches for multiple uses, and 18 to 24 inches for storing bulky items. It is best mounted on standards that allow adjustment to different heights. Shelving for chemical storage should be constructed of wood or other materials that resist corrosion and joined by plastic or plastic-coated connectors and shelf fittings. Lips on the edges of shelves increase safety for chemical storage and are mandatory in seismically active areas

When space is at a premium, the rolling compact shelf units often found in libraries may be used. These shelving units are lined up closely in rows until they are needed, at which time they are accessed by making use of the one aisle that serves the units. If these are to be used, a professional analysis of the loading capacity of the floor structure to determine loading capacity will be needed, because the units concentrate much higher

loads than fixed storage shelving. These units must be kept clamped to their rails at all times, except when they are in use. If they should break loose and roll freely, they will damage any wall they hit.

Today's trend toward micro-scale chemistry brings with it a reduction in the quantity of chemicals used. This increases safety and reduces the storage needs of the chemistry department. Teachers should always use stock bottles and prepare solutions outside the student area. Chemicals should never be stored in the classroom.

Separate ventilation should be provided for all rooms or closets in which chemicals are stored. All chemicals should be kept in dedicated, lockable cabinets or separate chemical storage areas. Chemicals must be divided into their compatible families, and incompatible chemicals are stored separately, with sufficient distance from each other. Secure, compact storage units for acids, flammables, and corrosives are available. Consult sources such as commercial catalogs for guidelines on storing chemicals, cleaning products, and flammables. In case of a fire or accident, a complete list of what is stored, together with material safety data (MSDS) sheets will be needed, and in some cases, required.

There is never sufficient storage space in science facilities. It is important to take inventory of all items that are being stored, not only to make better use of space, but as a serious safety concern, because old and forgotten materials can become explosive or produce unexpected hazards in a fire. Items that are no longer useful should be discarded safely or sent to authorized disposal facilities.

Rolling compact shelving. (100)

Storage cabinets in a laboratory. (101)

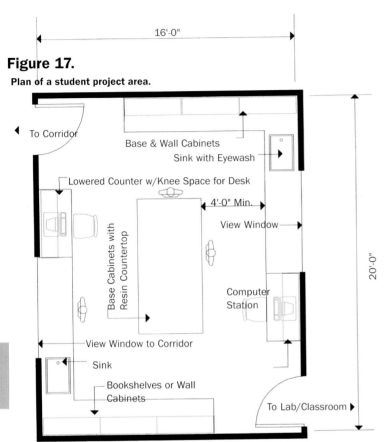

Figure 17.
Plan of a student project area.

16'-0"

To Corridor

Base & Wall Cabinets

Sink with Eyewash

Lowered Counter w/Knee Space for Desk

4'-0" Min.

View Window

Base Cabinets with Resin Countertop

Computer Station

20'-0"

View Window to Corridor

Sink

Bookshelves or Wall Cabinets

To Lab/Classroom

JTB

A very successful student project program on the East Coast is run in a converted carpentry shop in a large, open space with a high ceiling, lots of electrical power, water supplies, and floor drains. Tables and other apparatus are moved around as required.

Student Project Areas

The increasing emphasis on inquiry and individual and small-group work, as well as the guidelines suggested by the National Science Education Standards to increase students' capacities for conducting long-term investigations has resulted in a greater need for space for student projects. This space should be as close to the laboratory/classroom as possible. It is important to have a window between the two rooms or between the corridor and the student project room, to facilitate supervision. A door from the corridor will allow students and teachers to use the project space without disrupting nearby classes.

One practical layout is to place base cabinets with countertops, wall cabinets, and at least two sinks with hot and cold water around the perimeter. A central-island work area can be made from movable tables or additional base cabinets arranged back-to-back and covered with an epoxy resin countertop. Electric power with GFI-protected circuits and computer network connections should be installed along the perimeter and at the center island. If gas is used, the jets should be at the perimeter, and an emergency gas shut-off button will be necessary. Allow sufficient space between the perimeter counter and the center island so that students working at computer carts can access both work areas. The computer cart will require an aisle 4 or 5 feet wide.

Aquariums and terrariums for the observation, investigation, care, and cultivation of a variety of wildlife may be used as a design feature in the science area. Several new schools have large aquariums built into the walls of a student gathering space, where, in one instance, the aquarium is also visible from the adjacent laboratory/classroom. Terrariums can also be displayed in this manner.

A display system has been developed consisting of an adjustable shelving system with one glass wall and various shelving and lighting options. If it is installed as part of a corridor wall outside a science room, students and teachers passing by can see the displays of plants, animals, specimens, rocks, or equipment and observe the activities in the room.

Large aquariums require care and caution. Provide ample space and an electrical outlet with ground-fault protection.

Window into science. (102)

Grow Systems

A flexible area for student projects. (103)

Kathleen Sanner

For further information:

ADA requirements .... Chapter 3

Safety, fume hoods .... Chapter 3 & Appendix B

Outdoor facilities .... Chapter 7

Finishing materials .... Chapter 8

Projectors, screens, and other equipment .... Appendix D

Outdoor Facilities and Plant Windows

Access to natural settings is an important resource for a science program, even in urban environments, and especially at the elementary level. Wherever possible, the outdoor areas surrounding the school should be included in the facilities design plan. Providing nature trails, prairie grass areas, garden plots with various crops and herbs, and outdoor areas for weather balloon use and other investigations requires few physical facilities other than occasional tables, which may also be used for picnics.

One idea used successfully for a recent elementary and middle-level school was to arrange the shared building in a "doughnut" configuration, with a central courtyard providing a space that is used by both schools for outdoor activities.

Native Plantings

Careful planning during construction can help minimize disruption to existing plantings and any adverse impact on the natural communities. If a school has been built with little regard for the existing environment, native plantings can be established to restore some of the natural vegetation while providing windbreaks, shade, or other amenities. Planning, planting, and maintaining the school grounds can be a science project for all grades.

Models and Other Resources

Useful science models range from the complex and expensive, such as an elaborate stream with a wetland and waterfall, to the simple and inexpensive, such as animal footprints in a concrete sidewalk or a concrete strip with inset plaques representing the planets at their relative distances from the Sun. Other opportunities for outdoor scientific investigations include a weather station and stream tables to demonstrate stream erosion.

Weather station. (105)

Outdoor nature studies. (104)

Models of the planets set in concrete. (106)

Paw marks and fossils in concrete. (107)

A greenhouse as an extension of a lab. (108)

Greenhouses

A large window with shelves facing the sun provides a useful area for growing plants, a common hands-on activity at the elementary and middle-school levels. A simple, prefabricated plant window, 4 feet deep and 8 feet wide, with a glass roof can often be installed where there is an existing window with sufficient exposure to sunlight. The glazing should be of an insulating type that reduces heat gain while not filtering out the parts of the spectrum necessary for plant growth. Power will be needed for grow lights or shop lights, and a movable panel in the window or a separate exhaust fan can provide ventilation.

Greenhouses, whether simple or elaborate, are wonderful additions to a school's physical plant. Whenever possible, they should be located next to the science area. The more elaborate, full-sized greenhouses, which may be free-standing or attached to the building, often have evaporative coolers, hydroponics watering and feeding systems, and complex heating, ventilating, and shading mechanisms. One recently constructed high school has an appealing interior greenhouse with a pyramid roof structure on an upper level that catches the daylight and brings it into the interior space below.

A less expensive alternative to a stand-alone greenhouse that is also less demanding of electricity, heating, and air conditioning is a lean-to greenhouse attached to the walls of the classroom.

All of the above structures may be equipped with interior glass walls, grow lights, fan-type ventilation, water, drainage, and supplemental heat. Always check the direction and duration of sunlight at the chosen location for a greenhouse or plant window.

An economical structure for a greenhouse is a geodome covered by plastic sheeting.

An area for outdoor science. (109)

Ideas for Outdoor Displays and Resources

• Outdoor tap for hoses	• Weather balloons
• Outdoor sink	• Passive solar panels
• Thermometer	• Solar car race track
• Weather vanes	• Boulders of local rocks
• Sundials	• Model of the Solar System
• Bird feeders	• Fossils embedded in walls
• Cakes of lard for birds	• Geologic time line
• Nesting boxes for birds	• Model of the Earth
• Measured lengths in meters and yards	• Walls of sedimentary, metamorphic, and igneous rocks
• Inclined planes	• Pond

Interior of a greenhouse with a skylight. (111)

Outdoor classroom. (110)

Biodome. (112)

CHAPTER 8

Finishing Materials for Science Rooms

In selecting finishing materials, planners should consider that floors, walls, and ceilings in science rooms must be functional, durable, reasonably easy to maintain, and cost-effective.

Floors

Flooring materials should be chosen for easy maintenance and resistance to the chemicals that will be used in the room. Terrazzo (poured and polished concrete) is still the most durable flooring available for public buildings, but the cost is usually prohibitive. While carpet has attractive sound-absorbing and room-softening qualities, it is not a good choice for science classrooms or laboratories, particularly those where furniture will be moved around frequently. Chemical spills can damage or stain a carpet and make repairs a major problem. Dander from classroom animals and molds resulting from leaks remain embedded in carpets, causing health hazards.

Vinyl composition tile is a very good choice, because it resists wear and damaged areas can be replaced in small sections. Damaged tiles can be replaced easily in sections 12 inches square, from an overstock provided by the flooring contractor at the time of installation. Tiles, 1/8-inch thick, are the most widely used flooring materials in school science laboratories. They come in several formulations that vary in their ability to resist chemicals. The floor will have a lot of joints, but these are not visible once the floor has been installed and finished correctly.

Seamless or welded-seam resilient floors, particularly of the types developed for hospitals, perform well in science facilities, but they are much more expensive than vinyl composition tile and more difficult to repair, so they are normally considered only for high school laboratories. This type of flooring is nearly twice as expensive as the 1/8-inch vinyl composition tiles. The main advantage of these floors is that they resist staining and deterioration caused by most chemicals used in a school setting. The material comes in rolls, and the joints are heat-welded with matching strips.

The periodic table on the ceiling of a classroom. (113)

The resilient flooring may be rolled up the walls to form an integral base.

Fluid-applied composition flooring has also been proposed for science laboratories and classrooms. However, it is more expensive and harder than resilient flooring. This makes it difficult to patch, and it may crack if the underlying surface should move.

Animal models suspended from the ceiling. (114)

Ceilings

Ceilings may be made of suspended acoustic materials, to create the desired classroom environment and provide easy access to mechanical and electrical systems. If there is insufficient space to allow a suspended ceiling, interlocking square tiles, 12 inches on a side, may be glued directly to the deck above or to gypsum wallboard panels. Attention should be paid to the surface texture and plastic coating of the tile, particularly in rooms in which chemistry or biology will be taught. A tile surface that is deeply fissured is likely to become dirty from absorbed smoke. Plastic-coated acoustical tile that can be wiped down and resists some chemicals is available.

The science room's ceiling should be 10 feet high and can be used as a teaching tool. For example, one chemistry class recently stenciled the periodic table onto the ceiling tiles of their classroom. Other schools have used their ceiling suspension systems to display models of animals, fish, and birds.

Walls

Wall finishes in science rooms should be washable, durable, and easy to repair. School walls have long been built of very durable materials such as concrete block or plaster. These materials resist the damages of youthful exuberance, but provide no flexibility for running electrical and communications wiring and piping or for changing the space to meet new needs. Gypsum wallboard installed on metal studs offers this flexibility, but maintenance is needed whenever the surface is dented. Although wallboard repair is a simple and inexpensive process, other needs often take precedence, and the dented wallboard is not repaired.

Fiber-reinforced gypsum wallboard with an extremely durable surface is available and may be substituted for the standard gypsum board. This material costs about 80 percent more than standard wallboard. Installation costs are slightly higher, and may add 5 percent for a large job and up to 15 percent for a small one.

Heavy-duty, textured vinyl wallpaper over gypsum wallboard provides a durable surface that allows student work to be attached to it.

Some architects recommend using a thin coat of plaster on top of gypsum board lath, with a washable finished surface. Standard paint, with an eggshell or semi-gloss finish, works well and is easy to patch. Vinyl wall coverings also provide good surfaces, but are more difficult to patch than the paint. Hard surface finishes, such as epoxy paints, are difficult to patch, and probably not worth the extra expense for a school science room. Some recently formulated multicolor, spray-on, decorative finishes are easy to clean, but quite difficult to patch. Ground-faced concrete block is not recommended for science classroom walls, because it does not provide much flexibility and is difficult to clean.

Solar Energy for School Facilities

As demand for energy continues to grow, facilities planners should be aware of the possible applications of solar technology. Not only do solar energy systems help offset rising energy costs, but a well-designed facility may improve student performance and even add to the curriculum. Schools may go solar to solve a number of energy needs, from "daylighting" classrooms to reduce consumption of fossil fuels to cooling a classroom or heating water. In combination with other efficient energy resources, such as well-insulated walls and roofs and energy-efficient lighting, solar energy can provide significant savings over the long run.

Solar technology takes different forms, depending on institutional goals, site characteristics, budget, and other factors. Daylighting is a design-based strategy for bringing natural light into the interior of a building. A facility is constructed with most windows facing south to maximize daylight and may include skylights and "light shelves" that reflect window light into interior spaces. Not only does daylighting decrease the amount of electricity used for lighting, but it can also lower air conditioning needs, because the light fixtures produce less heat. Because of the amount of glass used, the main concerns associated with daylighting are heat gain during summer months and heat loss during the winter, which can be substantial in some regions. Such design strategies as overhangs above windows and shading systems over skylights help prevent the summer sun from entering the interior. Special window coatings and interior shades minimize heat loss through windows or skylights during the heating season.

In addition to lowering energy costs, daylighting provides a more comfortable light than fluorescent lighting. There is strong evidence that students perform better under natural light, as reflected in both attendance and test scores.

Passive solar technology uses the Sun for lighting and heating without the aid of mechanical or electrical devices. Heat is collected by thermal mass materials, such as masonry walls or roof ponds, and then released gradually during periods when the sun isn't shining.

The construction cost of a passive solar facility can run as much as or more than conventional building costs. Decreasing the size of heating and cooling systems saves in construction costs, however, and more savings are realized in the reduction in total energy use over time. Tests conducted by the National Energy Laboratory show that buildings with passive solar design use 47 to 60 percent less energy than those without.

Solar thermal systems use air or water heated by the sun as an energy source. In

A solar system for water and space heating. (115)

schools, solar-heated water can be used as is or can be run through other systems to heat or air-condition part of a building. Ferry Pass Middle School in Pensacola, Florida, supplies conditioned air to an 8,000-square-foot science wing, using solar thermal panels as a source of energy. Initial costs of such thermal systems are usually high, but operating costs are very low.

Solar photovoltaic (PV) systems rely on cells, usually made of silicon, to convert sunlight directly into electricity. These are commonly used to power calculators and wristwatches. More complex systems, consisting of arrays of cells anchored in panels, can generate electricity to pump water, power communications equipment, or heat a classroom, often at less cost than conventional electricity. PV panels, fixed or adjustable, can be mounted on the roof or on the ground. The number of panels needed depends on the wattage required. Generally, PV power is not practical for large electrical loads.

The primary obstacle to the use of solar panels is the high cost of the initial installation. However, recent cooperative ventures among utility companies, manufacturers, and state governments are making solar power more accessible to school systems around the country.

When schools use solar energy, they also provide students with learning opportunities. Solar energy systems can be incorporated in the curriculum to teach students the specifics of alternative forms of energy production, as well as data collection and measurement techniques.

There are many resources available both online and in print regarding solar energy and technology. A good place to start is with *Schools Going Solar*, a booklet produced collaboratively by the Interstate Renewable Energy Council (IREC), the Utility PhotoVoltaic Group (UPVG), and the American Solar Energy Society (ASES) (available online at http://www.eren.doe.gov/irec/programs/solarschools).

Reference
Schools Going Solar. (1998). Washington, DC: Interstate Renewable Energy Council, American Solar Energy Society, and Utility PhotoVoltaic Group.

Innovative Design

Skylights in a classroom. (116)

Building for Safety in Secondary School Science Facilities: A Survey*

Sandra S. West and Suzanne Lieblich

School _____

Classroom Teacher _____

Department Chair _____

Content Area _____

Please place a check mark in the appropriate column. "No" answers indicate a problem.

	YES	NO
I. Floor Space and Class Size		
A. 24 students or fewer per class (NSTA and NSELA recommendation)		
B. 60 sq ft/student floor space, minimum, for combination laboratory/classroom		
C. 45 sq ft/student floor space, minimum, for laboratory only		
D. 10 sq ft/student, minimum, preparation and storage space for teacher, including 1 sq ft/student, minimum, for chemical storage (240 sq ft for 24 students: eg, preparation and equipment storage room 8'x23', chemical storage room 8'x7')		
E. Additional space (approx. 20 sq ft) for lab station that meets ADA requirements		
F. Additional space for technological equipment (eg, approx. 15 sq ft per computer station, 10 sq ft for TV monitor with VCR or laser disc player, 12 sq ft for projector)		
G. Laboratory width 27 ft, minimum (preferably 30 ft)		
H. Aisles 4 ft wide, minimum, to allow students and teachers to move freely		
I. Doorways 36 in. wide, minimum		
II. Communication System		
A. Intercom or telephone in every room		
B. "Hot line" to office in every room (emergency telephone or intercom button)		
C. Accessible telephone located in every room or nearby (on same hall, less than 200 ft away)		
III. Shut-Off Controls		
A. Emergency shut-off controls accessible to teachers, preferably near the teacher's station, but not too easily accessible to students:		
1. Gas		
2. Electricity		
B. Master shut-off controls (if separate from emergency shutoffs) accessible to teacher, but not easily accessible to students		
C. All shut-off controls clearly labeled:		
1. Gas		
2. Electricity		
3. Water		

*Developed by Sandra S. West. Do not reproduce without giving credit to the authors.

	YES	NO

IV. Utilities

A. Vandal-resistant:

1. Gas jets

2. Water faucets

B. Electricity:

1. Sufficient number of electrical circuits provided in laboratory to meet needs of curriculum, including computer use

2. No DC lines (use small, dry cells for students or portable DC units for teachers, protected by circuit breakers or fuses)

3. All outlets in laboratory, preparation room, and storage room protected by ground-fault interrupters (GFI)

4. All outlets grounded and requiring 3-pronged plugs (OSHA requirement)

5. No outlets close to faucets or other water sources

6. Sufficient number of outlets provided to eliminate need for extension cords, overlapping wires, or plug-in outlet extenders (eg, 2 duplex outlets/lab station)

7. All laboratory refrigerators are spark-free

V. Fire Control and Security

A. ABC dry chemical fire extinguisher, or type required by local ordinance:

1. Present in every laboratory, preparation room, and equipment storage room

2. Present in every chemical storage room unless the room is attached to preparation/equipment storage room (may require more than one type of fire extinguisher to avoid chemical reactions)

3. In easily visible, unobstructed locations

4. Located near escape routes (second extinguisher may be in interior of room)

5. Correct size (5 lb, minimum, 16 lb, maximum, charge weight)

B. Access to fire exits (via doors and ground-floor windows):

1. 2 exits in every laboratory, with main door opening outward

2. 2 exits in every preparation room and equipment storage room

3. Fireproof doors that open outward for all chemical storage rooms

4. All exits labeled, unobstructed, and unlocked from inside

C. General alarm system for entire building

D. Smoke alarm present in every preparation room and equipment storage room

E. 2 smoke alarms in preparation/equipment storage room if 200 sq ft or larger

F. Smoke or heat alarm present in chemical storage room

G. Automatic sprinkler system (may be required under local or state fire codes):

1. Present in laboratory, preparation room, and equipment storage room

2. Recommended in chemical storage room (special head may be needed to protect against oxidation); water reactive chemicals require protected storage

3. No obstructions within 18 in. of ceiling

H. Lockable doors for all laboratories, preparation rooms, and storage rooms

	YES	NO
I. Safe entrance to roof, if roof-mounted weather station is to be used		

VI. Ventilation

	YES	NO
A. All room air vented to outside of building, not recirculated in building's ventilation system		
B. All exhaust air vented to outside of building, at sufficient distance from air intakes to prevent recirculation		
C. Laboratory ventilation at rate of 4 air changes/hr, minimum		
D. Preparation and equipment storage room ventilation at rate of 4 air changes/hr, minimum		
E. Chemical storage room ventilation:		
1. Continuous, with exhaust vented to outside of building		
2. At rate of 6 air changes/hr, minimum (OSHA requirement)		
F. Exhaust fan:		
1. Present in every laboratory, preparation room, and equipment storage room, for quick removal of excessive fumes		
2. Provided with manual control		
3. Exhaust vented to outside of building		
4. Equipped with fan guards, if wall-mounted		
G. Fume hood:		
1. Present in every laboratory where hazardous or vaporous chemicals are used		
2. Present in preparation room (may be single unit available to laboratory and preparation room, mounted on common wall)		
3. 2 fume hoods present in AP or advanced chemistry laboratory		
4. Exhaust vented to outside of building on roof or outside wall		
5. Located away from heavy traffic areas, doors and windows, and intake ducts		
6. Provides 80 to 120 linear ft, minimum, of air movement at hood face, for working with chemicals of low to moderate toxicity (ANSI Z9.5.7)		
7. Located at least 10 ft from main exit (ANSI Z9.5.4)		
8. Not located on a main traffic aisle (ANSI Z9.5.4)		
9. If shared by two or more fume hoods, ventilation system adequately engineered for purpose		
10. Sash level marked for 100 ft of air movement and with date of measurement		
11. Meets ASHRAE 110 testing standard (at least 4.0 AU 0.10)		
12. Not used as storage area		
H. Laboratory ventilation meets ANSI Z9.5 standard		

VII. Lighting

	YES	NO
A. 50 fc/sq ft, minimum, general lighting level in laboratory, preparation room, and storage rooms		

	YES	NO

B. 75 fc/sq ft, minimum, on counter surfaces underneath wall cabinets

C. Battery-operated emergency light:

  1. Present in every laboratory, storage room, and preparation room that has insufficient natural light or is used at night

  2. Located next to doorway in laboratory and preparation room

VIII. Work Areas

A. All work surfaces made of chemical-resistant materials

B. In laboratory:

  1. 6 linear ft work space/student (including counters and flat tables)

  2. 6 linear ft counter space adjacent to a large sink

  3. 1 sink/4 or 5 students, sinks 15"x15", minimum, with flexible, chemical-resistant mats (such as neoprene)

  4. Hot water available

  5. Heat source available

  6. Electricity with GFI-protection provided

C. In preparation/equipment storage room:

  1. 4 linear ft, minimum, counter space, adjacent to a large sink, 16"x20" minimum

  2. 9 linear ft, minimum, counter space (total; 12 linear ft preferable)

  3. Hot water available

  4. Heat source(s) available

  5. Electricity with GFI-protection provided

D. Clear floor space for laboratory carts, AV equipment, human skeleton, etc

E. Area(s) for safety equipment in every laboratory and preparation room:

  1. Space near fire extinguisher for safety equipment such as sand container and fire blanket

  2. Space for safety equipment such as first-aid kit and poster, chemical waste container, and spill kit

  3. Space for hanging aprons for 24 students (in laboratory or preparation room)

IX. Equipment for Personal Protection

A. Eyewash:

  1. Provided in every laboratory, within 25 ft of all workstations

  2. Unobstructed

  3. Eyewash (preferably dual eyewash, which treats both eyes simultaneously) located near safety shower (squeeze bottle and single eye drench not sufficient)

  4. Dual eyewash in every chemistry and physical science laboratory and every classroom, laboratory, and preparation room where hazardous chemicals are used

  5. Dual eyewash provides instant, gentle, tempered flow of aerated water for 15 minutes, and preferably can stay in open position, leaving user's hands free

	YES	NO

B. Safety shower:

1. Available in every chemistry and physical science laboratory, within 50 ft of all workstations

2. Unobstructed shower and valve handle

3. Fixed valve pull handle (no chains unless provided with large ring)

4. Sufficient water pressure (20 psi, minimum, for 68 gal/min)

5. Floor drain with trap present

C. Eyewashes and safety showers meet ANSI Z358.1 standard

D. At least one eyewash and safety shower accessible to students with disabilities (see below)

E. Safety features for equipment (such as belt guards on belt-driven machinery) provided

X. Storage
A. Chemicals:

1. Storage in secure, regulated areas, with entry only for authorized personnel

2. No storage in classroom or areas to which students have access

3. No storage of hazardous chemicals in preparation room, equipment storage room, or rooms with sensitive equipment or electrical outlets

4. Sufficient space for safe, specialized storage:

a. Space for storing chemicals with sufficient distance between incompatible chemicals, preferably with impermeable partitions

b. Vented, corrosion-resistant (non-metal or coated metal) cabinet for storing acids, with corrosion-resistant shelves and supports

c. Separate cabinet for nitric acid, away from other acids and readily oxidized substances

d. Dedicated, grounded, and approved cabinet or safety cans for storing flammables separately

e. Lockable cabinet for poisons

f. Protected location for water-sensitive chemicals, especially to shield from water sprinklers

5. All shelves equipped with lip edge or rod to prevent bottle roll-off

6. Shelves made of wood with plastic supports, or other corrosion-resistant materials

7. Shelves for chemical containers 12 in. deep (maximum), so containers will not be stored more than 2 containers deep

8. Sufficient shelf space available so chemicals can be reached easily and will not be knocked over

9. Laboratory refrigerator in preparation room, spark-free to protect against flammables

10. Only chemical-resistant countertops

B. Gas cylinder: (Compressed gases are not normally used in secondary school science. Numerous safeguards are necessary, including the following. See American Chemical Society, 1995, pp. 14-15.)

1. Chained to prevent from falling over and from becoming a missile if it develops a leak (with chain securely fastened to a stud or other wall support)

		YES	NO
2.	Can be clamped tightly into place after being positioned for use		
3.	Stored away from heat or ignition source		
C.	Cabinets in laboratory and preparation and storage rooms:		
1.	Ample for storage needs, including at least one tall cabinet		
2.	Secured to floor and/or wall with sufficient attachments to keep from falling		
3.	Some lockable cabinets provided, to prevent theft of equipment		
4.	Solid doors (no glass fronts)		
D.	Open shelves in laboratory and preparation and storage rooms:		
1.	Ample for storage needs, in a variety of depths (12 to 24 in.)		
2.	Equipped with lip edges or rods in earthquake-prone areas		
3.	Hanging shelves secured to wall or ceiling with sufficient attachments to keep from falling		
4.	Hanging shelves solid enough to support a substantial amount of weight		
E.	Space in preparation room or equipment storage room for:		
1.	Protective clothing (safety goggles, aprons, etc)		
2.	Carriers of chemicals and acids		
3.	Large items and equipment, such as supply carts, safety goggles sanitizer, and microscopes		

XI. Adaptations for Students with Disabilities

		YES	NO
A.	Permanent laboratory station or space for portable laboratory station (with gas, if used, electricity, water, sink, and sockets for rods) that meets ADA guidelines		
B.	Accessible controls (eg, levers or electronic controls) for gas, electricity, and water		
C.	Adapted seating at counter, table, or desk:		
1.	Counter/table/desk height 34 in., maximum (26 to 30 in., recommended, for students under 12 years old)		
2.	Vertical knee clearance 27 in., minimum (24 in., minimum recommended, for students under 12 years old)		
D.	Adapted sink:		
1.	Counter height and sink rim 34 in. above floor, maximum (30 in., maximum recommended counter height, and 31 in., maximum recommended sink rim height, for students under 12 years old)		
2.	Sink depth 6 1/2 in., maximum		
3.	Vertical knee clearance 27 in., minimum (24 in., minimum recommended, maximum for students under 12 years old), with protection from hot water pipes		
4.	Accessible controls		
E.	Accessible eyewash and safety shower:		
1.	Distance from wall to center of eyewash bowl 17 to 24 in.		
2.	Eyewash spout 36 in. above floor, maximum (30 in., maximum recommended, for students under 12 years old)		
3.	Shower pull handle 44 to 54 in. above floor, depending on shower's location and whether it can be accessed from side or only from front		

	YES	NO
F. Adapted fume hood in chemistry and physical science laboratory (seating, controls, knee space)		
G. Aisles 36 in., minimum, and doorways 32 in., clear width minimum, for wheelchair clearance		
H. 5' diameter turning space for wheelchair		
I. Wiring for electronic aids, such as field monitors for hearing-impaired students		
J. No protruding upper cabinets or sharp corners on cabinets, for vision-impaired students		

Recommendations

Acronyms

ADA	Americans with Disabilities Act
ANSI	American National Standards Institute
ASHRAE	American Society of Heating, Refrigerating, and Air-Conditioning Engineers
NFPA	National Fire Protection Association
NSELA	National Science Education Leadership Association
NSTA	National Science Teachers Association
OSHA	Occupational Safety and Health Administration

References

American Chemical Society, Committee on Chemical Safety. (1995). *Safety in Academic Chemistry Laboratories* (6th ed.). Washington, DC: Author.

American National Standards Institute. (1990). *Emergency Eyewash and Shower Equipment* (ANSI Standard Z358.1-1990). New York: Author.

American National Standards Institute. (1992). *Laboratory Ventilation* (ANSI Standard Z9.5-1992). New York: Author.

American Society of Heating, Refrigerating, and Air-Conditioning Engineers. (1985). *Method of Testing Performance of Laboratory Fume Hoods* (ANSI/ASHRAE Standard 110-1985). Atlanta, GA: Author.

Architectural and Transportation Barriers Compliance Board. (1992). *Americans with Disabilities Act Accessibility Guidelines for Buildings and Facilities.* Washington, DC: Author.

National Fire Protection Association. (1997). *Life Safety Code* (NFPA Standard 101). Quincy, MA: Author.

National Science Education Leadership Association. (1998). *NSELA Handbook.* Marblehead, MA: Author.

National Science Teachers Association. (1998). *NSTA Handbook: 1998–99.* Arlington, VA: Author.

Occupational Safety and Health Administration. (1910). *Design and Construction of Inside Storage Rooms* (General Industry Standard 29 CFR 1910.106 OSHA 2206).

Table of Critical Dimensions

ITEM	GRADES K–2	GRADES 3–5	MIDDLE SCHOOL	HIGH SCHOOL	REMARKS
TABLES					
Dimensions of Tabletop	30" x 30"	24" x 48"	24" x 54"	24" x 54"	Flat-topped tables recommended
Seating Height	18" to 20"	21" to 23 "	25" to 30"	30"	29" preferable for h.s. biology
COUNTERS					
Depth	24", min.	24", min.	24", min.	24", min.	30" min. for map drawers
Height	24"	27"	32" to 36"	36"	ADA height 34", max.*
Knee Space (Horizontal)	24", min.	24", min.	24" to 30"	30"	ADA 30", min.*
Knee Space (Vertical)	18", min.	20", min.	22" to 26"	26"	ADA 27", min.*
SINKS					
Depth	8", min.	8", min.	8", min.	8", min.	ADA sink depth 6.5", max.*
Height	24"	27"	32" to 36"	36"	ADA height 34", max.*
"Rinseaway" Sink Length	70 1/2"	70 1/2"	70 1/2" to 114"	70 1/2" to 114"	
BASE CABINETS					
Height	22 1/2"	25 1/2"	30 1/2" to 34 1/2"	34 1/2"	Under 1 1/2"-thick counter
Depth	21 1/2"	21 1/2"	21 1/2"	21 1/2"	Under 24"-deep counter
					27" min. depth for map drawers
WALL CABINETS					
Depth	12" to 15"	12" to 15"	12" to 15"	12" to 15"	
Mounting Height:	18" above counter	18" above counter	18" above counter	18" above counter	
Students	42"	45"	52" to 54"	54"	ADA height 48", max.*
Adults	54"	54"	54"	54"	ADA height 48", max.*
COMPUTERS (DESKTOP)					
Station Area	15 sq ft	15 sq ft	15 sq ft	15 sq ft	Includes cart and seated student
Minimum Cart Size	21" D x 30" W	21" D x 30" W	21" D x 30" W	21" D x 30" W	
Chair plus Student	36" D	36" D	36" D	36" D	
Aisle Space for Cart	60"	60"	60"	60"	Front of cart to objects behind seat

*ADA requirement for adults.

ITEM	GRADES K–2	GRADES 3–5	MIDDLE SCHOOL	HIGH SCHOOL	REMARKS
COMPUTERS (LAPTOP)					
Surface Area	10" x 12"	10" x 12"	10" x 12"	10" x 12"	Reserved counter space not required
Storage Cabinet for Laptops	15" D x 30" W x 30" H	15" D x 30" W x 30" H	15" D x 30" W x 30" H	15" D x 30" W x 30" H	Cabinet 15" deep holds 20 laptops
PREPARATION ROOM					
Minimum Size	8' x 12'	8' x 12'	8' x 12'	8' x 12'	8' x 16' desirable for m.s. and h.s.
Size of Teacher's Desktop	72" W x 29" to 30" H	72" W x 29" to 30" H	72" W x 29" to 30" H	72" W x 29" to 30" H	
SHELVING DEPTHS					
For Books	10", min.	10", min.	10", min.	10", min.	
For Equipment Storage	12" to 24", mixed	12" to 24", mixed	12" to 24", mixed	12" to 24", mixed	12" max. for chemicals, some at 30" for physics
AISLE SPACE					ADA 36" min. for continuous aisle
Between Tables	24" to 36"	24" to 36"	24" to 36"	24" to 36"	36" is preferable for safety
Between Tables and Counters	48"	48"	48"	48"	48" min. around perimeter of room
Between Tables and Marker Board	8'	8'	8'	8'	10' pref. for projector use
PROJECTION SCREEN					
Minimum Size	5' H x 7' W	5' H x 7' W	5' H x 7' W	5' H x 7' W	6' H x 8' W is preferable
SHOWER/EYEWASH					
Eyewash Bowls (Height)	24"	25" to 26"	38"	38"	ADA eyewash spout height 36", max.*
Shower Handles (Height)	N/A	N/A	68"	68"	ADA height 54", max., if side access*
FUME HOODS					
Deck Height	N/A	N/A	32" to 36"	36"	ADA height 34", max.*
LIGHTING					
General	50 fc, min.	50 fc, min.	50 fc, min.	50 fc, min.	Glare-free lighting recommended
At Work Surface	75 to100 fc	75 to100 fc	75 to100 fc	75 to100 fc	Glare-free lighting recommended

*ADA requirement for adults.

ITEM	GRADES K–2	GRADES 3–5	MIDDLE SCHOOL	HIGH SCHOOL	REMARKS
MARKER BOARD					
Minimum Width	12'	12'	16'	16'	Multiple sliding panels recommended
Mounting Height:					
Students	24"	27"	32" to 36"	36"	
Adults	36"	36"	36"	36"	
BULLETIN BOARD					
Minimum Width	6'	6'	6'	6'	
Mounting Height:					
Students	24"	27"	32" to 36"	36"	
Adults	36"	36"	36"	36'	
FLOOR SPACE					
Minimum per Student:					
Multiple-Use Classroom	45 sq ft	45 sq ft	N/A	N/A	
Science Room or Laboratory Only	40 sq ft	40 sq ft	45 sq ft	45 sq ft	
Laboratory/Classroom	N/A	N/A	60 sq ft	60 sq ft	
STORAGE SPACE					
Minimum per Student:					
For Chemicals	1 sq ft	1 sq ft	1 sq ft	1 sq ft	Included in 10 sq ft prep. and storage
For Preparation and Storage	10 sq ft	10 sq ft	10 sq ft	10 sq ft	
CEILING HEIGHT	10'	10'	10'	10'	
DOORWAY WIDTH	36", min.	36", min.	36", min.	36", min.	ADA 32" min. clear width for wheelchair clearance

*ADA requirement for adults.

Equipment

Projectors and Screens

Projection screens should be mounted on walls or ceilings. Their dimensions should be at least 5 by 7 feet, but 6 by 8 feet is preferable. Remember to specify additional sections, or "tails," at the top of screens that are to be attached to high ceilings. The bottom of the screen will then be approximately 4 feet above the floor. Using marker boards as projection screens is not advisable, because their surfaces do not reflect light well.

Apply the following formula to determine if your video monitors are adequate to serve your lecture area: The diagonal dimension of the monitor, in inches, is equal to the maximum viewing distance, in feet. This figure also indicates the number of students that can view the screen comfortably. The angle between the line of sight and the screen should not be greater than 45 degrees.

A liquid crystal display (LCD) projector may be mounted on a rolling cart together with a videocassette recorder and videodisc player. Outlets centered about 12 to 16 feet from the projection screen can supply electricity, cable TV wiring, and computer input to the projector. The size of the projected image will be 6 by 8 feet. Images from a video camera connected to a microscope eyepiece can also be projected through the LCD projector.

The emergence of LCD projectors has made TV monitors less popular. However, a good television monitor with a VCR costs $600 to $800, whereas the cost of an LCD projector that projects computer and video output is much higher—beginning at about $3,000. Large-screen televisions are expensive, not as flexible as the LCD projectors, and they produce lower resolution images than computer monitors or LCD projectors.

There are several systems for projecting images onto a screen:
- a conventional slide projector
- a VCR and television screen
- a video camera connected to a microscope and LCD projector or television screen
- an LCD projector connected to a VCR or computer
- an overhead projector

Approximate Cost of Equipment, in 1998 $US

Screen (6' x 8')	$100 to $500
Conventional slide projector	$200 to $1,300
Large-screen television	$900
Video camera with microscope adapter	$1,000
Microscope	$100 to $900
Liquid crystal display (LCD) projector	$3,000 to $6000
Videocassette recorder	$200 to $600
Overhead projector	$400
Microprojector	$700

Planning for Equipment Purchases

It is almost impossible to plan the ordering of loose equipment for science programs during the construction process. However, in order to be ready for move-in day, some orders must be prepared ahead of time.

When ordering start-up supplies, outline the 10 or 20 most crucial laboratory experiences for a class and document everything you will need in order to offer those experiences. Remember the supplies that are often taken for granted, such as pencil sharpeners, paper towel dispensers, brooms, and dustpans. A new facility will have nothing!

The following lists are for discussion purposes. Costs are rounded to the nearest dollar. They are representative, and not specific product sale prices. The sample lists are based on a class of 24 students, with laboratory setups for each group of four students. Although the number of students in a class should not exceed 24, equipment for 28 is ordered, to cover breakage and loss. These lists may be useful when you are submitting plans to committees for their consideration.

The lists are not complete, and are meant as starting points. Consumables are not listed, because they are seldom included in construction budgets and they vary with the curricula.

Another area not addressed is decorative furnishings for walls. The periodic table is just the beginning: display boards, clocks, and mirrors are essential. Murals of scientific phenomena are popular. Be creative. Schools are no longer the drab institutions they once were.

Safety Equipment for Every Classroom

Item	Number per Class	Representative Cost
Acid cabinet	1	$ 600
Fire blanket	1	$ 100
First aid Kit	1	$ 50
Fire extinguisher ABC	1	$ 40
Spill control center	1	$ 400
Safety shield	1	$ 125
Goggles	29	$ 90
Goggles sanitizer	1	$ 500
Heat and acid resistant gloves	29	$ 200
Aprons	29	$ 350
Safety handbooks	2	$ 250
Safety/chemical inventory software	1	$ 100
Hot hand holder	8	$ 100

List of Suppliers for Laboratory Furniture and Equipment

For a listing of suppliers, please refer to the Equipment/Supplies section of the *NSTA Supplement of Science Education Suppliers*.

For your convenience, the Equipment/Supplies section of the guide has been made available online at http://www.nsta.org/scisupp/guide.htm. The entire guide may be purchased from NSTA by calling (800) 722–NSTA.

General Equipment: Chemistry or Physical Science

Item	Number per Class	Representative Cost
Electronic balances	8	$2500
Anti-theft locks for balances	8	$ 200
Triple beam balance	8	$ 800
Auxiliary masses for balances	8	$ 400
Hot plates	8	$1200
Autoclave/sterilizer	1	$3500
Centrifuge	1	$ 300
Flasks/erlenmeyer 125/250/500/1000 ml	140 per size	$1000
Corks/rubber stoppers for flasks	280 per size	$ 840
Clamps/test tube and extension	40/16	$ 240
Volumetric flasks 100/500 ml	42 per size	$1400
Rimless test tubes (OD X Lmm) (6 x 50) (13 x 100) (18 x 150)	72 per size	$ 100
With corks to fit	72 per size	$ 25
Funnels/short and long stemmed	36	$ 180
Microscale chemistry kits (test plates and spatulas)	8	$ 150
Pipettes/volumetric 1 ml/5 ml/10 ml	24 per size	$ 450
Thermometers	40	$ 200
Spectrophotometer with tubes and lamps	1	$1000
TI Calculator-based lab systems	8	$2000
TI Calculator for overhead	1	$ 300
Interface probes for calculator based labs, temperature/pH/ micropressure	8 each	$2400

General Equipment:
Life Science

Item	Number per Class	Representative Cost
Electronic balances	8	$2500
Aquarium /40 gallon complete	1	$ 500
Monocular compound microscopes 4x/10x/40x with in stage condensers	8	$2500
Binocular stereoscopic microscopes	8	$2500
Hot plates	8	$1200
Autoclave/sterilizer	1	$3500
Dissection pans and kits	15	$ 300
Flasks/erlenmeyer 125/250/500/1000 ml $250	35 per size	
Corks for flasks	70 per size	$ 210
Slides and cover slips	720	$ 50
Slide survey sets	8 per type	$ 160
Volumetric flasks 100/500ml	14 per size	$ 450
Plant grow light/station	1	$ 600
Funnels /short- and long-stemmed	36	$ 180
Pipettes/volumetric 1 ml/5ml/10 ml	24 per size	$ 450
Rimless test tubes (OD X Lmm) (6 x 50) (13 x 100) (18 x 150) plus corks to fit	72 per size	$ 100 / $ 25
Petri dishes	80	$ 200
Electrophoresis cell and power supply	1	$ 700
TI calculator-based lab systems	8	$2000
Interface probes for calculator based labs, temperature/pH/carbon dioxide	8 each	$2400

General Equipment
Physics

Item	Number per Class	Representative Cost
Electronic balances	8	$2500
Power supplies ac/dc	8	$2000
Optics light bench	8	$3200
Laser/modulated 0.8mW	1	$ 500
Hot plates	8	$1200
Oscilloscope	8	$4800
Photogate timers	15	$1500
Triple-beam balances	8	$ 800
Thermometers	15	$ 75
Spectrophotometer with tubes and clamps	1	$1000
Test tubes and (OD/Lmm) 18 x 150 Corks	72 / 72	$ 30 / $ 15
Volumetric flasks 100/500ml	14 per size	$ 450
Meter sticks	16	$ 50
Stop watches	16	$ 160
Vernier calipers	8	$ 80
Clamps, extension (universal)	24	$ 200
Pulleys	16	$ 50
TI calculator-based lab systems	8	$2000
TI calculator for overhead	1	$ 300
Interface probes for calculator-based labs, temperature/pH/pressure/light	8 each	$3000

Sample Checklists

Elementary Science

Category	Guidelines	Good	Fair	Poor	Comments
Is there adequate floor space for the students to work safely?	40 sq ft minimum per student for science room; 45 sq ft minimum for multiple-use classroom Sufficient space between desks. 4 ft aisles				
Is the space flexible?	Rectangular room without alcoves				
Is there room for open floor activities and demonstrations?	Room 30 ft wide, minimum Movable student tables Movable teacher's table				
Is there adequate space for the teachers?	Secure storage and desks Space available to teacher during planning time.				
Is the power supply adequate and safe?	Ground-fault interrupters Sufficient circuits and outlets to serve program and technology needs				
Is the lighting adequate?	Directed and diffused to avoid glare 50 foot-candles, minimum per sq ft 75–100 foot-candles at work surface				
Can lighting levels be controlled?	Separate switches for rows of lights Room-darkening shades or blinds				
Is there safe and adequate storage?	10 sq ft per student for teacher's storage and preparation space Secure storage Space for lab and AV equipment				
Is there a good infrastructure for communications?	Telephone for emergencies Network wiring for computers Cable for video communication				
Are there counters or tables for investigations?	Counters 36" high for adults, 24" for grades K–2, 27" high for grades 3–5 Tables 18–20" high for grades K–2, 21"–23" high for grades 3–5				
Is there a water supply suitable for investigations?	1 sink at adult level, at least 1 per 6 students (K–2), 1 per 5 students (3–5), at student's level Swivel and high-arched faucets, deep bowls				
Is there adequate space for displays?	Counter and floor space Shelves and display cabinets Many easily reached tackboards				
Is there space to keep living organisms?	Shelves at windows for plants Grow lights Terrariums or aquariums				
Does the space meet ADA requirements?	At least one wheelchair-accessible counter and sink Accessible safety equipment, doors, and passages				
Are fire and safety measures in place?	Fire and safety equipment, eyewash Adequate fire exits Adequate room ventilation and exhaust fan				

Adapt and expand upon the categories and guidelines in this checklist to suit your program's needs. See Chapters 3 and 4 for detailed suggestions.

SAMPLE CHECKLIST

Middle School Science

Category	Guidelines	Good	Fair	Poor	Comments
Is there adequate floor space for the students to work safely?	45 sq ft min per student for laboratory; 60 sq ft min for combination laboratory/classroom. Sufficient space between desks. 4-ft aisles				
Is there adequate space for the teachers?	Teacher's space with secure storage and desk, not in shared classroom				
Is the power supply adequate and safe?	Ground-fault interrupters. Sufficient curcuits and outlets to serve program and technology needs. Sufficient outlets at lab stations				
Is the lighting adequate?	Directed and diffused to avoid glare. 50 foot-candles, min, per sq ft. 75–100 foot-candles at work surface				
Can lighting levels be controlled?	Separate switches for rows of lights. Room-darkening shades				
Is there safe, adequate storage and a secure place for chemicals?	10 sq ft per student for teacher's storage and preparation space. Separate, lockable room or closet. Space for separation of incompatible chemicals				
Is the preparation space adequate and secure?	Lockable preparation room, preferably at least 8' x 16'				
Is there a good infrastructure for communications?	Telephones for emergencies. Network wiring for computers. Cable for video. Television or LCD projector. Room-darkening shades or blinds				
Are there counters or tables for investigations?	Counters 36" high for adults, 32"–36" high for students. Tables 25"–30" high for students. Movable lab tables or fixed lab stations				
Is there a water supply suitable for investigations?	At least 1 sink per 4 students at students' level, a large sink. Swivel and high-arched faucets. Deep bowls				
Is there space to keep living organisms?	Greenhouse or window shelves for plants. Terrariums or aquariums				
Is there a separate space for small-group and individual student projects?	Student project room with view-window or adequate space arranged to facilitate supervision. Safety equipment and GFI-protected outlets				
Is there space for long-term investigations?	Student project room with holding space for long-term projects. Space for investigations in the classroom				
Does the space meet ADA requirements?	At least one wheelchair-accessible workstation. Accessible safety equipment, doorways, and passages				
Are fire and safety measures in place?	Fire and safety equipment. Adequate exits				
Are there exhaust fans to vent smoke and fumes?	Exhaust fans are vented to outside of the building				
Are a safety shower and eyewash provided where chemicals are used?	Dual eyewash within 25 ft of every workstation if hazardous chemicals are used. Eyewash and shower available for simultaneous use				

Adapt and expand upon the categories and guidelines in this checklist to suit your program's needs. See Chapters 3 and 5 for detailed suggestions.

SAMPLE CHECKLIST

High School Science

Category	Guidelines	Good	Fair	Poor	Comments
Is there adequate floor space for the students to work safely?	45 sq ft min per student for laboratory; 60 sq ft min for combination laboratory/classroom Sufficient space between desks. 4-ft aisles				
Is there adequate space for the teachers?	Teacher's space with secure storage and desk, not in shared classroom				
Is the power supply adequate and safe?	Ground-fault interrupters Sufficient circuits and outlets to serve program and technology needs				
Is the lighting adequate?	Directed and diffused to avoid glare 50 foot-candles, minimum per sq ft 75–100 foot-candles at work surface				
Can lighting levels be controlled?	Separate switches for rows of lights Room-darkening shades or blinds				
Is there safe, adequate storage and a secure place for chemicals?	10 sq ft per student for teacher's storage and preparation space Separate, lockable room or closet Adequate space for separation of incompatible chemicals				
Is the preparation space adequate and secure?	Lockable preparation room, preferably at least 8'x16'				
Is there a good infrastructure for communications?	Telephones for emergencies Network wiring for computers Cable/or video communication Television				
Are there counters or tables for investigations?	Adult-height counters and tables Movable lab tables or fixed lab stations Epoxy resin work surfaces				
Is natural gas or other heat source available?	Natural gas or hot plates 1 service per 4 students Safety shutoff in classroom				
Is there a water supply suitable for investigations?	At least 1 sink per 4 students, 1 large sink Swivel and high-arched faucets, deep bowls Hot (max 120°F) and cold water				
Is there adequate space for displays?	Shelves and display cabinets				
Is there a separate space for small-group and individual student projects?	Room with view window or adequate space arranged to facilitate supervision GFI-protected outlets				
Is there space for long-term investigations?	Student project room with holding space for long-term projects Space in the classroom				
Does the space meet ADA requirements?	At least one wheelchair-accessible workstation Accessible safety equipment, doorways, and passages				
Are fire and safety measures in place?	Fire and safety equipment Adequate exits Adequate ventilation Exhausts vented to outside of building				
Is a fume hood provided where it is required?	Fume hood required if hazardous chemicals are used Fume hood vented to outside of building				
Are a safety shower and eyewash provided?	Dual eyewash within 25 ft of every workstation if hazardous chemicals are used Eyewash and shower available for simultaneous use				

Adapt and expand upon the categories and guidelines in this checklist to suit your program's needs. See Chapters 3 and 6 for detailed suggestions.

APPENDIX F

Photograph Credits

1. LaMoine L. Motz
2. National Research Council, National Academy of Sciences
3. LaMoine L. Motz
4. Kathe Engster
5. William Bishop
6. Fisher Hamilton
7. Juliana Texley
8. M. Moody
9. William McComas
10. Sandra S. West
11. Fisher Hamilton
12. CampbellRhea
13. CampbellRhea
14. Presidential Awards
15. James T. Biehle
16. James T. Biehle
17. James T. Biehle
18. Sheldon Laboratory Systems
19. James T. Biehle
20. James T. Biehle
21. James T. Biehle
22. James T. Biehle
23. James T. Biehle
24. James T. Biehle
25. James T. Biehle
26. James T. Biehle
27. James T. Biehle
28. James T. Biehle
29. James T. Biehle
30. James T. Biehle
31. James T. Biehle
32. James T. Biehle
33. *Science Scope*
34. T. Kokoski, L. Schaffer, H. Pinson

35. James T. Biehle
36. James T. Biehle
37. Patricia Strawbridge
38. James T. Biehle
39. James T. Biehle
40. James T. Biehle
41. James T. Biehle
42. James T. Biehle
43. William Baczkowski
44. James T. Biehle
45. James T. Biehle
46. James T. Biehle
47. James T. Biehle
48. James T. Biehle
49. James T. Biehle
50. James T. Biehle
51. Juliana Texley
52. James T. Biehle
53. James T. Biehle
54. James T. Biehle
55. James I. Biehle
56. James T. Biehle
57. James T. Biehle
58. James T. Biehle
59. James T. Biehle
60. M. B. Hoover
61. Jane B. Nelson
62. Fanning Howey Associates
63. James T. Biehle
64. James T. Biehle
65. James T. Biehle
66. Patricia Strawbridge
67. James T. Biehle
68. James T. Biehle
69. Fisher Hamilton

70. Ernest Schiller
71. James T. Biehle
72. Fisher Hamilton
73. James T. Biehle
74. James T. Biehle
75. James T. Biehle
76. James T. Biehle
77. Fisher Hamilton
78. James T. Biehle
79. Stepen Cashman
80. James T. Biehle
81. James T. Biehle
82. Ellen Ebert
83. James T. Biehle
84. James T. Biehle
85. James T. Biehle
86. James T. Biehle
87. Fisher Hamilton
88. Presidential Awards
89. James T. Biehle
90. James T. Biehle
91. James T. Biehle
92. James T. Biehle
93. Stephen Cashman
94. James T. Biehle
95. LaMoine L. Motz
96. James T. Biehle
97. James T. Biehle
98. James T. Biehle
99. William Baczkowski
100. James T. Biehle
101. James T. Biehle
102. Grow Systems
103. Kathleen Sanner
104. James T. Biehle

105. James T. Biehle
106. James T. Biehle
107. James T. Biehle
108. James T. Biehle
109. James T. Biehle
110. Presidential Awards
111. B. Jefferey Stebar
112. Biospaces
113. James T. Biehle
114. James T. Biehle
115. North Carolina Solar Center
116. Innovative Design

Glossary of Construction Terms

ABC extinguisher—A fire extinguisher for use on all general sources of fire: "A" sources (burning paper, wood, trash, etc), "B" sources (burning flammable liquids), and "C" sources (electrical fires).

Architect—A person licensed to perform architectural services, from analysis of project requirements and creation of a project design to general administration of the construction contract.

Building permit—A permit required by most municipalities before new or significant renovation construction can proceed and is-sued to the owner and the general contractor. Application usually involves the architect's submission of a complete set of design draw-ings and calculations to be reviewed for com-pliance with local building codes.

Casework/Cabinetwork—Cabinets, counters, shelves, and other woodwork.

Change order—A written order to the con-tractor authorizing a specific change in the work from that described in the original con-struction contract.

Conduit—Plastic or metal tubing through which wire is pulled for electrical power, tele-phone lines, data connections, and other uses.

Construction contingency—An allowance in a construction budget to cover the costs of changes resulting from circumstances that cannot be predicted, such as the need to re-move buried trash or deal with unsatisfactory soils. The allowance should be a minimum of 5 percent of the estimated construction cost, and is often greater.

Construction cost—The amount to be paid to the general contractor for construction of the project, including change orders. When a construction manager is employed, the con-struction cost is the sum of all trade construc-tion contracts, including change orders.

Construction documents—The products prepared by the architect and engineering con-sultants that will be used by the general con-tractor as directions for constructing the facil-ity. Typically, they consist of drawings, which may include plans, elevations, details, sec-tions, and schedules, and technical specifica-tions that describe the products and construc-tion techniques to be used.

Construction management—A form of project delivery in which the owner contracts with a construction manager to perform cer-tain services during the design phase and to manage the construction process.

Construction manager (CM)—A firm hired by the owner to provide advice on costs, scheduling, and constructibility during the design phase and to coordinate the work of various trade contractors during construction of a project. The construction manager may be a general contractor or a professional con-sultant.

Contingency fund—A fund additional to the construction budget that covers unforeseen changes in projected costs. *See* Design con-tingency and Construction contingency.

Design/bid/build—The traditional linear process in which the owner hires an archi-tect, who designs the project and assists the owner in obtaining bids for the construction of the project. The design must be completed before bidding and construction take place. During construction, the architect adminis-ters the construction contract and observes the work in progress as an agent of the owner.

Design/build—A process in which the owner awards a contract to a firm or group of firms to design and build a construction project for a fixed price. The owner must first prepare a comprehensive and detailed set of requirements, including a program, usually with the help of an architect.

Design contingency—An allowance in a construction budget that provides for needed items that will be incorporated into the project before bidding takes place, but which are unknown at the time the budget is established. The design contingency should be approximately 10 percent of the construction cost as estimated before design work has begun.

Downlight—A light fixture that aims light downward. Downlights are often recessed into the ceiling.

Drywall—*See* Wallboard.

Dual eyewash—An emergency eyewash that is designed to wash both eyes simultaneously and operates in such a way that the victim has both hands free to hold his or her eyes open.

Educational specifications—The requirements set forth by a school district that guide the architectural design, such as the general size and nature of the spaces for particular activities. The object of educational specifications is to express the needs of the educational program so that the facilities to be designed and constructed will meet those needs.

Engineering consultant—A specialized firm or individual with expertise in a particular area of construction engineering. Typical specialties include civil, structural, mechanical, and electrical engineering. This consultant is usually a subcontractor to the architect.

Epoxy—Epoxy resin, a member of a class of resins used in adhesives, coatings, and castings.

Eyewash—A fixture that provides streams of water to flush the eyes in case of emergency. Often combined with safety shower.

Fiberoptic cable—Glass fibers in a protective sheath used for the transmission of telephone, television, or computer data signals. Fiberoptic cables transmit data much faster than copper wire and can conduct many different signals simultaneously.

Fire marshal—A state or local official whose responsibility is to assist owners and architects in designing facilities that have the appropriate conditions for fire safety. Generally, the fire marshal gives advice and direction to the parties during the design phase and reviews the final construction documents for compliance with local and national fire protection regulations. Consulting the fire marshal early in the planning process of a project can greatly improve the safety of the result and minimize time-consuming design changes when applying for a permit.

Foot-candle (fc)—A measure of illumination on a surface that is equivalent to that produced by one candle at a distance of one foot; equivalent to one lumen per square foot.

General conditions—A term that has two meanings in the context of a construction project: 1. The written requirements in the agreement between the owner and the general contractor that identify the responsibilities of the various parties to the agreement and delineate details such as insurance to be carried. 2. Cost items involved in a construction project that do not become incorporated directly into the project, such as a job-site trailer, dumpsters, and temporary telephone. The general contractor will include a budget for these expenses in the bid.

General contractor (GC)—A firm hired by the owner to build the project. Many general contractors conduct a portion of the construction, such as the concrete work and carpentry, and issue subcontracts to other trade contractors to perform the balance of the work under the supervision and coordination of the general contractor.

Geotechnical investigation—Underground investigation by a geotechnical engineer to predict as accurately as possible the conditions below the ground surface. The results can direct the location of a new building and the design of its foundations.

Glazing—Panes or sheets of glass or other transparent or translucent material, often set in frames or windows.

Grading—The process of reshaping the slope and contours of a building site to accommodate the design of a facility. Depending on the site and the proposed project, grading may be minor or may become a major project in itself, involving blasting to remove rock or importing loads of soil to fill low areas.

Ground-fault interrupter (GFI)—A circuit breaker, usually located in a socket, used to prevent injury from contact with electrical equipment by shutting off power before damage caused by a ground fault can occur. Required in locations where one might be in contact with a grounded surface and an electrical source, particularly adjacent to a water supply.

Grow light—A fluorescent light bulb that emits light conducive to plant growth.

Gypsum—A common mineral used to make plaster and wallboard.

Hazardous materials survey and abatement—Identification of all locations in which hazardous materials used in past construction may exist within the facilities, and a plan for removing or encapsulating these materials so as to eliminate the hazard. In a renovation project, it is likely that some hazardous materials will be removed from a building before construction begins.

Joist—A horizontal section of wood, steel, or concrete framing, spanning between beams or bearing walls, and used to support a raised floor.

Landscaping—Trees, shrubs, and other plantings on a building site.

Lath—A thin wood or metal strip or mesh used to support plaster.

Life-cycle costs—The cost of owning and operating a building through its useful life, including construction, interest on borrowed money, maintenance, fuels, electricity, periodic repairs, replacement of equipment or finishes, and the ultimate demolition of the building. These costs can be reduced by good design and careful selection of building materials and systems.

Lumen—A unit of light emitted from a single source, equal to the light falling on one square foot of surface of an imaginary sphere with a one-foot radius around one candle.

Material Safety Data Sheet (MSDS)—A reference describing the known hazardous properties of a particular chemical and precautionary measures to be taken when using it. The usual sources of MSDS sheets are chemical suppliers.

Movable equipment—Nonexpendable movable items such as tables, LCD projectors, carts, and laboratory equipment.

Off-site construction costs—Costs for necessary construction on the property of others, such as bringing a water main to the site, connecting a sewer main to the nearest public sewer, and road improvements on adjacent roadways.

Program—A listing of spaces required to satisfy the needs of a particular architectural project, including the overall area, dimensions, physical requirements of each space and the relationship of each space to all other spaces. The program is often developed by the architect through interviews with the users of the facility and becomes the guideline for the architectural design of the facility.

Punch list—A list of incomplete construction items, generally minor in nature, prepared by the architect or general contractor when a construction project is substantially complete for owner occupancy.

Safety shower—A shower fixture for washing chemicals off a person in an emergency to minimize injury.

Schematic design—The initial design phase of a construction project, in which the architect translates the requirements of the program into a physical concept. A schematic design will display in graphical form the various spaces, their relationships to one another, and how they will work together as a building. Drawings of the exterior appearance of the building are also prepared as part of the schematic design.

Shop drawings—Detailed drawings for the manufacture of items fabricated off site. The drawings are generally prepared by the manufacturer for review by the architect.

Site development costs—Costs in addition to the building construction costs, which may include clearing and grading, roads, parking lots, utility construction, and retaining walls.

Site survey—Survey of the existing conditions on the site, showing the location, bearing, and dimensions of the property lines, any easements, the topography of the land, location and elevation of any structures on the site, and the location and elevation of existing utility lines. The architect needs an accurate site survey in order to develop an accurate design.

Space program—*See* Program.

Specifications—A written document, prepared by the architect, describing the materials, methods, and other details of the proposed construction, furniture, or equipment. The specifications complement the construction drawings.

Subcontractor—A trade contractor who has a contract with the general contractor to perform a specific portion of the construction project for the general contractor. The subcontractor is paid by the general contractor.

Substantial completion—The stage in the progress of the work when the work is complete in accordance with the contract documents to the extent that the owner can occupy or use the work for its intended purpose.

Suspended ceiling—A ceiling system suspended beneath overhead structural framing and often concealing heating and air-conditioning ductwork, piping, electrical conduits, and the structure itself.

Trade contractor—A specialty construction contractor who will perform a specific portion of a construction project as a subcontractor to a general contractor. When the owner employs a construction manager, the term may also refer to a firm that has a direct contract with the owner to perform a specific portion of the construction. Examples of trade contractors include roofing, plumbing, and painting contractors.

Troffer—A trough-shaped reflector that holds fluorescent lamps.

Value engineering—An objective, systematic method of obtaining optimal costs for a facility over a specific number of years, considering the costs of construction, operations, maintenance, and replacement.

Wallboard— Interior wall and ceiling surfacing material, generally consisting of gypsum sandwiched between sheets of paper.

Warranty period—A period of time (usually one year) following the final completion of a construction project during which the general contractor must repair deficiencies and correct work that does not conform to the requirements of the contract documents.

Bibliography

American Association for the Advancement of Science. (1990). *Project 2061: Science for All Americans.* New York: Oxford University Press.

American Association for the Advancement of Science. (1991). *Barrier Free in Brief: Laboratories and Classrooms in Science and Engineering.* Washington, DC: Author.

American Chemical Society. (1993). *Safety in the Elementary (K–6) Science Classroom.* Washington, DC: Author.

American Chemical Society, Committee on Chemical Safety. (1995). *Safety in Academic Chemistry Laboratories* (6th ed.). Washington, DC: Author. (Single copies are available without charge to school science administrators and teachers)

Americans with Disabilities Act Accessibility Guidelines for Buildings and Facilities. (1991, July 26). *Federal Register, 56*(144).

Architectural and Transportation Barriers Compliance Board. (1992). *Americans with Disabilities Act Accessibility Guidelines for Buildings and Facilities.* Washington, DC: Author.

Baughman, James, Jr., and Zollman, Dean. (1977). Physics Lab for the Blind. *The Physics Teacher, 15*(6), 339–42.

Biehle, James T. (1995, May). Complying with Science. *American School and University, 67*(9), 54–56. (Discusses accessibility issues in science laboratories)

Biehle, James T. (1995, November). Six Science Labs for the 21st Century. *School Planning and Management, 34*(9), 39–42.

Biehle, James T. (1997, February). Four Keys to Putting Tomorrow's Technology in Yesterday's Buildings. *School Planning and Management, 36*(2), 27–28.

Biehle, James T. (1997, March). Tomorrow's Science in Yesterday's Buildings. *AIArchitect, 4,* 527–31.

Biehle, James T. (1997, Summer). A New Approach to Campus Construction. *Planning for Higher Education, 25,* 31–35.

Brennan, J. W. (1970). *An Investigation of Factors Related to Safety in the High School Science Program.* Dissertation, University of Denver. (ERIC Document Reproduction Service No. ED 085 179)

California Department of Education, Science and Environmental Education Unit. (1993). *Science Facilities Design for California Public Schools.* Sacramento, CA: Author.

Collins, B. Kevin. (1985, May). One Person's Trash. *Science and Children, 22*(8), 17.

Cooper, E. Crawley. (1994). *Laboratory Design Handbook.* New York: CRC Press.

Dell'Isola, Alphonse J. (1974). *Value Engineering in the Construction Industry.* New York: Construction Publishing Co.

DiBerardinis, Louis J., Baum, Janet S., First, Melvin W., Gatwood, Gari T., Groden, Edward F., and Seth, Anand K. (1993). *Guidelines for Laboratory Design: Health and Safety Considerations* (2nd ed.). New York: Wiley/Interscience.

Emergency Eyewash and Shower Equipment (ANSI Standard Z358.1-1990). (1990). New York: American National Standards Institute.

Fire Protection for Laboratories Using Chemicals (NFPA Standard 45). (1996). Quincy, MA: National Fire Protection Association.

Flinn Biological Catalog/Reference Manual. (1996). Batavia, IL: Flinn Scientific, Inc. (Contains advice on safety in the laboratory)

Flinn Chemical Catalog/Reference Manual. (1996). Batavia, IL: Flinn Scientific, Inc. (Contains advice on safety in the laboratory)

Flinn, L. C., III. (1993). Overcrowding in the Science Laboratory. *Flinn Fax!, 93*(1), 4–5. (Newsletter available from Flinn Scientific, Inc., P. O. Box 219, Batavia, IL 60510)

Florida Department of Education. (1992). *Barrier Free in Brief: Laboratories and Classrooms in Science and Engineering: A School Science Safety Manual.* Tallahassee, FL: Author.

Florida Department of Education. (1992). *Science Safety: No Game of Chance! A School Science Safety Manual.* Tallahassee, FL: Author.

Florida Department of Education. (1993). *Science for All Students: The Florida Pre K–12 Science Curriculum Framework.* Tallahassee, FL: Author.

Fox, Peggy. (1994, January). Creating a Laboratory: It's Elementary. *Science and Children, 31*(4), 20–22.

General Services Administration, Department of Urban Housing, Department of Defense, and United States Postal Service. (1988). *Uniform Federal Accessibility Standards.* Washington, DC: U.S. Government Printing Office.

Gerlovich, J. A. (Ed.). (1984). *School Science Safety: Elementary School.* Batavia, IL: Flinn Scientific.

Gerlovich, J. A. (Ed.). (1984). *School Science Safety: Secondary School.* Batavia, IL: Flinn Scientific.

Governor's Committee on High School Science Laboratories for the 21st Century. (1992). *Look of the Future: Report of the Governor's Committee on High School Science Laboratories for the 21st Century.* Baltimore, MD: State of Maryland, Public School Construction Program.

Grocoff, Paul N. (1996). *Effects of Correlated Color Temperature on Perceived Visual Comfort.* Dissertation, University of Michigan, College of Architecture and Urban Planning. (Available from University Microfilms, 1-800-521-3042)

Harbeck, Mary B. (1985, October). Getting the Most Out of Elementary Science. *Science and Children, 23*(2), 44–45.

Heintschel, R. M. (1982). *Science in Ohio's Secondary Schools: A Status Report.* Columbus, OH: Ohio State Department of Education. (ERIC Document Reproduction Service No. ED 224 708)

Hill, Franklin. (1988). *Tomorrow's Learning Environment: Planning for Technology: The Basics.* Alexandria, VA: National School Boards Association.

Jbelly, Kamil A. (1990). *On Providing a Safe and Effective Science Learning Environment: Safety Practices/Conditions and Accreditation.* Austin, TX: Texas Education Agency.

Justrite Manufacturing Co. (1985). *How to Handle Flammable Liquids Safely.* Des Plaines, IL: Author.

Kaufman, James A. *The Kaufman Letter.* Natick, MA: James A. Kaufman and Associates. (Newsletter on safety issues, available from 192 Worcester Road, Natick, MA 01760)

Krajkovich, Joseph G. (1983). *A Survey of Accidents in the Secondary School Science Laboratory.* Edison, NJ: New Jersey Science Supervisors Association.

Laboratory Safety Workshop. (1976). *Laboratory Safety Guidelines: 40 Suggestions for a Safer Laboratory.* Natick, MA: Author. (Available from the organization's web site at http://www.labsafety.org/)

Laboratory Ventilation (ANSI Standard Z9.5-1992). (1992). New York: American National Standards Institute.

Lien, Vi, and Skoog, Gerald. (1983). Survey of Texas Science Education. *Texas Science Teacher, 18*(2), 5–17.

Life Safety Code (NFPA Standard 101). (1997). Quincy, MA: National Fire Protection Association.

Los Angeles, Orange, and San Diego County Offices of Education. (1989.) *Remodeling and Building Science Instruction Facilities in Elementary, Middle, Junior, and Senior High Schools.* Downey, CA: Los Angeles County Office of Education. (Also available from Orange County Department of Education, in Costa Mesa, and San Diego County Office of Education)

Lowery, Lawrence F. (Ed.). (1997). *NSTA Pathways to the Science Standards: Elementary School Edition.* Arlington, VA: National Science Teachers Association.

Macomber, Robert D. (1961). Chemistry Accidents in High School. *Journal of Chemical Education, 38*(7), 367–368.

Madrazo, Gerry M., Jr., and Motz, LaMoine L. (Eds.). (1993). *Sourcebook for Science Supervisors* (4th ed.). Arlington, VA: National Science Teachers Association.

Maryland State Department of Education, School Facilities Branch. (1994). *Science Facilities Design Guidelines.* Baltimore, MD: Author.

Means Building Construction Cost Data 1999 (54th ed.). (1998). Kingston, MA: R. S. Means.

Mehlville School District Senior High School Model: Science. (1992). St. Louis, MO: Sverdrup Corporation.

Method of Testing Performance of Laboratory Fume Hoods (ANSI/ASHRAE Standard 110-1985). (1985). Atlanta, GA: American Society of Heating, Refrigerating, and Air-Conditioning Engineers.

Mione, Lawrence V. (1995). *Facilities Standards for Technology in New Jersey Schools.* Trenton, NJ: New Jersey Department of Education.

Narum, Jeanne L. (Ed.). (1995). *Structures for Science: A Handbook for Planning Facilities for Undergraduate Natural Science Communities, Volume III.* Washington, DC: Project Kaleidoscope.

National Council on Schoolhouse Construction. (1964). *Guide for Planning School Plants.* East Lansing, MI: Author.

National Research Council, National Academy of Sciences. (1996). *National Science Education Standards.* Washington, DC: National Academy Press.

National Science Teachers Association. (1993). *Safety in the Elementary Science Classroom* (Rev. ed.). Arlington, VA: Author.

National Science Teachers Association. (1993). *Scope, Sequence, and Coordination of Secondary School Science: Vol. 1: The Content Core* (Rev. ed.). Arlington, VA: Author.

National Science Teachers Association. (1998). Laboratory Science (1990 position statement). In *NSTA Handbook 1998–99* (pp. 194–197). Arlington, VA: Author.

National Science Teachers Association Task Force on Science Facilities and Equipment. (1993). *Facilitating Science Facilities: A Priority*. Arlington, VA: National Science Teachers Association.

North Carolina Department of Public Instruction, Division of Science Education. (1991). *Hints on Science Room Design*. Raleigh, NC: North Carolina Public Schools.

North Carolina Department of Public Instruction, Division of School Planning. (1991). *North Carolina Public Schools Facility Standards: A Guide for Planning School Facilities*. Raleigh, NC: North Carolina Public Schools.

North Carolina Department of Public Instruction, Division of School Planning. (1992). *North Carolina Public Schools Furnishing and Equipment Standards: A Guide for Planning and Equipping New Facilities and Evaluating Existing Schools*. Raleigh, NC: North Carolina Public Schools.

Occupational Safety and Health Administration. (1910). *Design and Construction of Inside Storage Rooms* (General Industry Standard 29 CFR 1910.106 OSHA 2206).

Rakow, Steven J. (Ed.). (1998). *NSTA Pathways to the Science Standards: Middle School Edition*. Arlington, VA: National Science Teachers Association.

Reese, Kenneth M. (Ed.). (1985). *Teaching Chemistry to Physically Handicapped Students* (Rev. ed.). Washington, DC: American Chemical Society.

Schools Going Solar. (1998). Washington, DC: Interstate Renewable Energy Council, American Solar Energy Society, and Utility PhotoVoltaic Group. (Available on-line at http://www.eren. doe.gov/irec/programs/solarschools)

Showalter, Victor M. (Ed.). (1984). *Conditions for Good Science Teaching*. Arlington, VA: National Science Teachers Association.

Steele, Marilyn M., Conroy, Paul A., and Kaufman, James A. *There's No Safety in Numbers*. Natick, MA: Laboratory Safety Workshop. (Review of state-by-state rules on class sizes)

Summerlin, Lee. (1995). *A to Z Safety in the Elementary Science Classroom* (2nd ed.). Birmingham, AL: Alabama Science Teachers Association.

Texas Administrative Code. School Facilities Standards. Title 19, Part II, Chapter 61, Subchapter CC, §61.1033. (Available on-line at www.sos.state.tx.us/tac/index.html/)

Texas Education Agency (TEA). (1989). *Planning a Safe and Effective Science Learning Environment*. Austin, TX: Author.

Texley, Juliana, and Wild, Ann. (Eds.). (1996). *NSTA Pathways to the Science Standards: High School Edition*. Arlington, VA: National Science Teachers Association.

Wang, Denis. (1994, February). A Working Laboratory. *The Science Teacher, 61*(2), 26–29.

Ward, John. (1992, September). Shopping for Science. *The Science Teacher, 59*(6), 28–33.

Ward, Susan, and West, Sandra S. (1990, May). Accidents in Texas High School Chemistry Labs. *The Texas Science Teacher, 19*(2), 14–19.

Ward, Susan, and West, Sandra S. (1990, May). Science Laboratory Safety Survey. *The Texas Science Teacher, 19*(2), 9–13. (Written with Carolyn J. Pesthy)

West, Sandra S. (1991, September). Lab Safety. *The Science Teacher, 58*(6), 45–49.

West, Sandra S., and Pesthy, Carolyn J. (1987). *Science Lab Safety Survey*. (Safety checklist available from Southwest Texas State University, San Marcos, TX, web site: http://bluebonnet.bio. swt.edu)

Young, John R. (1970). A Survey of Safety in High School Chemistry Laboratories of Illinois. *Journal of ChemEd, 47*(12), A829–838.

Young, John R. (1971). The Responsibility for a Safe High School Chemistry Laboratory. *Journal of ChemEd, 48*(5), A349–356.

Young, John R. (1972). A Second Survey of Safety in Illinois High School Laboratories. *Journal of ChemEd, 49*(1), 55. (Contains research on space necessary for science safety in the laboratory)

Young, Jay A. (Ed.). (1991). *Improving Safety in the Chemical Laboratory: A Practical Guide* (2nd ed.). New York: Wiley/Interscience.

Young, Jay A. (1997, March). Chemical Safety, Part I: Safety in the Handling of Hazardous Chemicals. *The Science Teacher, 64*(3), 43–45.

Young, Jay A. (1997, April). Chemical Safety, Part II: Tips for Dealing with Laboratory Hazards. *The Science Teacher, 64*(4), 40–41.

Young, Jay A., Kingsley, Warren K., and Wahl, George H. (1990). *Developing a Chemical Hygiene Plan*. Washington, DC: American Chemical Society.